USBORNE TRUE STORIES

SPIES

This edition published in 2007 by Usborne Publishing Ltd,
Usborne House, 83-85 Saffron Hill, London
EC1N 8RT, England.
www.usborne.com

A catalogue record for this title is available
from the British Library

Printed in the UK

Series editors: Jane Chisholm and Rosie Dickins
Designed by Brian Voakes
Series designer: Mary Cartwright
Cover design by Michael Hill
Illustrations by Peter Ross

USBORNE TRUE STORIES

SPIES

PAUL DOWSWELL &
FERGUS FLEMING

CONTENTS

This charming man...

Everyone liked Gordon Lonsdale – the handsome Canadian seemed to have friends all over London. In the late 1950s his face was familiar in the capital's best clubs and restaurants, and his car, an expensive white model imported from America, made a splash in a country still recovering from the hardships of World War Two. He lived in a beautiful apartment block called "The White House", just by Regent's Park. Here, he gave extravagant parties and charmed a succession of girlfriends attracted to his dark good looks.

Behind the playboy image, though, Lonsdale was a hard-working businessman. He ran a company which leased jukeboxes, vending machines and car security equipment. His work took him all over the country. But there was yet another side to the playboy businessman – one that would have astonished every single girlfriend, business associate and restaurant owner who thought they knew him well. His real name was Konon Trofimovich Molody and he was a Soviet spy.

Molody had led an extraordinary life. He was born in Russia in 1922, but he had been sent to live with an aunt in California when he was only seven years old. Nine years later, he spoke English like a native. Returning to Russia in 1938, he joined the Communist Youth Movement and fought heroically during World War Two. When the war ended Molody was recruited by the KGB, the Soviet Union's security service. He had a fanatical faith in his country's communist ideology and a brilliant flair for languages — two major qualifications that would make him an ideal spy.

By the age of thirty two, he had reached the rank of commander and had been sent on numerous foreign missions. In 1954, with Cold War hostility between the Soviets and Western enemies such as the United States and Britain approaching a peak, he was given his most important mission yet.

A new form of warfare had developed after World War Two — submarines carrying nuclear missiles. Such vessels lurked unseen beneath the seas of the world. Impossible to track and destroy, they were capable of inflicting nuclear destruction on their nation's enemies. Molody was to be sent undercover to Britain, to discover all he could about the Royal Navy's nuclear submarines, which were among the most advanced in the world. To do this he would have to establish contacts with other Soviet spies, and find members of the British armed services or government who would be prepared to sell him such secret information.

An assignment like this asked a great deal of an agent. Molody was now thirty three. He would have to leave everything he possessed in the Soviet Union behind him, and go to live in a foreign land as a total stranger. He was given a new identity and nationality – that of Gordon Lonsdale. There had been a Canadian named Gordon Lonsdale, but he had disappeared in Finland – possibly murdered – and his doctored passport, and past life history, was now in Molody's hands. He was sent to Canada in 1954. After a year living his life there as Lonsdale, he arrived in Britain in March 1955. He was to play out his new identity extraordinarily well.

❖

Gordon Lonsdale had two very good friends out in London's western suburb of Ruislip – Peter and Helen Kroger. A quiet American couple in their 50s, they ran a business dealing in antique books. One time, friends on the street asked them to a dinner party. Helen arrived wearing a long black dress, and their hostess exclaimed: "Why Helen, you look like a Russian spy!" If she hadn't been laughing so much at her own little joke, she would have seen the Krogers exchange a terrified glance. Helen Kroger was indeed a Russian spy, and so was her husband. Their house at 45 Cranley Drive was a major threat to British security.

Under the kitchen floor was a cavity containing a high-frequency transmitter and a high-speed tape recorder for sending coded messages at more than 240 words a minute. An internal 23m (74ft) antenna stretched into and around the attic. In the sitting room was a radio which could receive signals from anywhere in the world. Beside it stood a typewriter, tape recorder and some headphones. The bathroom could be converted into a photographic darkroom, complete with a gadget for making and reading microdots – a technology which could reduce large photographs to a size smaller than a pinhead.

There were surprises everywhere. A copy of the Bible in the sitting room concealed light-sensitive cellophane for making microdots. In the bedroom was a microscope for studying them. Rolls of microfilm were hidden in a hipflask. In the bathroom, a container of powder unscrewed to reveal a microdot reader rather like a small telescope. A large cigarette lighter on the table concealed a secret compartment full of coded messages.

The Krogers had led lives just as extraordinary as Molody's. Peter Kroger had been born Morris Cohen, of Russian-Jewish parents in New York. He met and married Helen at the University of Illinois. Her real name was Leona Petka. During the 1930s both had become communists, and Peter had gone to fight against the fascists in the Spanish Civil War. He had returned to the United States and worked for various Soviet trade organizations there before serving in the American army in World War Two.

After the war the couple began to spy for the Soviet Union, and helped to pass on American atomic bomb secrets to the Russians. They fled from America in 1950, suspecting they were about to be arrested, and surfaced again in Britain in 1954. This time they were known as the Krogers, having taken their identity and backgrounds from a New Zealand couple who had died earlier in the century.

❖

Lonsdale was a frequent visitor to Cranley Drive – he came to dinner at least one Saturday of every month. Of course that was not all he did. The Krogers were Lonsdale's link with the Soviet Union. It was there, in their quiet suburban house, that the fruits of his spying work were transmitted to the KGB in Moscow.

Lonsdale's best contact was a Royal Navy clerk at the top-secret Admiralty Underwater Weapons Establishment in Portland, Dorset. His name was

Harry Houghton. He had access to a variety of "classified" (secret) material, and better still for Lonsdale, he had a shady past. In 1951 he had been posted to the British Embassy in Warsaw, Poland. There he had disgraced himself by keeping a mistress and dealing in black market goods. He was sent home with a severe reprimand. Yet despite his suspect character, he had been posted to Portland.

The British authorities were not the only ones keeping tabs on Harry Houghton in Warsaw. The Polish secret service had been watching him too. They told the KGB he was likely to be easily corruptible. The KGB passed on this titbit to Lonsdale, who wasted no time introducing himself.

Lonsdale told Houghton he was Commander Alex Johnson from the American Embassy. As they chatted away, he realized Houghton was just the man he needed. He was willing to do almost anything for money. It was easy to trick him into becoming a traitor. Lonsdale said the Americans needed certain information from him. He need not worry about the Official Secrets Act – a document guaranteeing confidentiality that all armed forces personnel were required to sign – after all, weren't Britain and the United States on the same side?

When Lonsdale mentioned money, Houghton's eyes lit up. He also came up with a clever scheme for smuggling documents out of Portland. Houghton had a girlfriend at the base, a middle-aged woman named Ethel "Bunty" Gee. She was a filing clerk with high level security clearance – meaning she handled top secret documents. Although there were spot checks on male employees as they came in and out of the building, to make sure they were carrying no secret documents, female staff were never searched. This bizarre lapse in security meant that Bunty would be a perfect accomplice.

Soon all sorts of files, from charts of navy docks to details of shipbuilding projects, were being smuggled out of Portland. Their contents were dictated onto a tape recorder, then transmitted in high speed radio bursts from Cranley Drive, or they were photographed to be smuggled on to Moscow as microfilm. Then Bunty returned them before anyone noticed they were missing. It all worked like a dream. Lonsdale and the Krogers were able to smuggle secrets on from Houghton and Gee, as well as other military and intelligence organization contacts they had made, for six years.

❖

But all good things come to an end. Houghton may have been Lonsdale's best source, but he was probably also the most unreliable person the Soviet spy had to deal with.

Routine checks by MI5 – Britain's counter-intelligence agency – showed that the Portland navy clerk was living way beyond his means. In 1960 his official earnings were only £714 – a modest salary at the best of times. Yet he had just bought a flashy new car, laid out £10,000 on a house, and was spending £20 a month on drink alone. Where was this money coming from? MI5 were determined to find out. Checks on Houghton's bank account gave nothing away though. Lonsdale paid him in cash, so the police would never be able to trace the source of this new-found wealth back to him.

In July 1960 an MI5 operative started to tail Houghton and Gee. He followed them on a trip to London, to the Old Vic theatre in Waterloo. He watched them meet Gordon Lonsdale, who handed over an envelope in exchange for a grocery bag. Then Houghton and Gee left, taking an odd, roundabout route back to their car. It was all highly suspicious.

Then a month later, Houghton went up to London again. Here he met Lonsdale at the Old Vic, and the two of them retired to a café. The MI5 man slid into the table next to theirs and strained to hear the conversation.

"These will be the first Saturday in each month," said Lonsdale, "especially the first Saturday in October and November."

Something was definitely being planned.

They left the café, and the MI5 man followed at a distance. Then, both men crammed into a phone booth. But instead of making a call, Houghton gave Lonsdale a file wrapped in a newspaper. Then they parted. Houghton disappeared into the crowd, but the MI5 man followed Lonsdale, who got into a car and drove off. Another couple of MI5 men followed him in their own car and watched him as he stopped outside a bank. He got out, handed over a brown suitcase to a bank official, and drove off.

After he had gone the MI5 men moved in. They discreetly explained to the bank manager that they were employed by the government on work of a highly sensitive nature, and that they needed to look inside the suitcase. The manager understood, and they found that Lonsdale's case contained a Russian-made camera, a magnifying glass, two films and an assortment of keys. It was all very curious.

Then there was a lull in investigations. Lonsdale went away to Europe for two months on business, but when he returned from his trip, MI5 agents were waiting for him. They tailed him as he picked up the suitcase from the bank, and then got on a train to Ruislip.

Over the next few weeks, as MI5 watched, a pattern emerged. On the first Saturday of each month, Houghton would meet Lonsdale in London.

They would exchange packages, and that evening Lonsdale would go to Ruislip, arriving at the Kroger's house about 7:15pm. After three months MI5 decided to swoop. The man in charge of the operation was Detective Superintendent George Smith of London's Special Branch police force.

❖

On January 7, 1961, Harry Houghton made his journey to London. On this occasion Bunty Gee came with him, carrying a big shopping bag. They arrived at Waterloo Station where no less than 15 agents, including George Smith, loitered on the platform disguised as passengers and newspaper sellers. The train was 45 minutes late. Maybe it was the delay that made Smith's men sloppy, maybe it was the cold. Whatever the reason, they were taken by surprise when the couple reached the station exit and dashed for a bus. Only one man managed to get on the bus with them.

Houghton and Gee had taken a spur-of-the-moment sightseeing trip, and after an hour or two they returned to Waterloo Station and went over to the Old Vic theatre, as they usually did. Here Smith's men were waiting for them again. Lonsdale was waiting there too, to greet them. When they arrived, he took Gee's bag, as if making a gentlemanly gesture of carrying it for her. That was enough for Smith. He ran up to all three and said: "I'm a police officer, and you're all under arrest."

At that instant, three unmarked cars screeched to a halt in front of them all. Lonsdale was bundled into the first, Houghton the second, and Gee the third. The cars sped off, and a pre-arranged radio signal was sent out: "Lock, stock and barrel." All three had been grabbed without so much as a shout in anger.

Gee's bag was certainly full of interesting items. There were four files from Portland and film containing more than 300 photographs of top-secret material on British nuclear submarines.

At the police station all three were charged under Britain's Official Secrets Act. Their responses varied dramatically.

Harry Houghton was crestfallen: "I've been a bloody fool!" he blurted.

Bunty Gee was indignant: "I've done nothing wrong," he protested.

Gordon Lonsdale was as cool as a cucumber: "As I appear to be going to stay here all night, could you find me a good chess player?"

His request was granted.

(While Lonsdale was in custody, Smith would ensure there was always a first-class chess player among his guards. Smith admired Lonsdale's style, and explained his generous attitude to newspaper journalists, saying: "He had a difficult job to do – so do you and so do I. He did it well. How can I condemn a man for that?")

❖

Later that afternoon Peter and Helen Kroger also received unexpected visitors. Smith and his squad hurried up to Ruislip as soon as Houghton, Gee and Lonsdale were safely in custody. When the police arrived to arrest them, the Krogers were quite calm. They acted as if this visit from the police must be a mistake but, as any decent citizens would do, they were prepared to cooperate fully until they were released.

As they left the house, however, Helen Kroger asked for permission to stoke the boiler for the night, so that the house would be warm when they returned. Smith, who was nobody's fool, said: "Certainly, Mrs. Kroger, but first let me see what's in your handbag."

Helen Kroger looked stony faced. This was the moment she must have realized the game was up. In the bag were typed messages, a glass slide containing three microdots and a five page letter, written in Russian by Lonsdale. This was all intended for the boiler, but now it would become prime evidence for the prosecution case against them instead.

With all five members of Lonsdale's spy ring now under arrest, the police unleashed forensic squads on all of their homes. Naturally, it was 45 Cranley Drive that revealed the most incriminating clues to their activities. The radio and microdot equipment were easily located, but over the next week, as the house was virtually dismantled, police investigators found signal codes, transmission dates, thousands of US dollars, two New Zealand passports in the name of the Krogers, and two Canadian passports as well. Lonsdale's apartment revealed a radio set and microdot equipment, and Harry Houghton and Bunty Gee's respective homes contained equally incriminating secrets – including official documents, a camera and a box of matches with a false-bottom, which held a map of meeting places in London.

The trial started on March 13, 1961, and went on for nine days. Newspapers dubbed the spies "The Microdot Five." All were found guilty of spying and sentences were duly handed out. Houghton and Gee got 15 years each, the Krogers got 20 years. Lonsdale was clearly perceived to be the man in charge of the spy ring and the judge reserved the stiffest sentence for him.

"Gordon Arnold Lonsdale," he said, "you are clearly a professional spy. It is a dangerous career and one in which you must be prepared, as no doubt you are, to suffer. You will go to prison for 25 years."

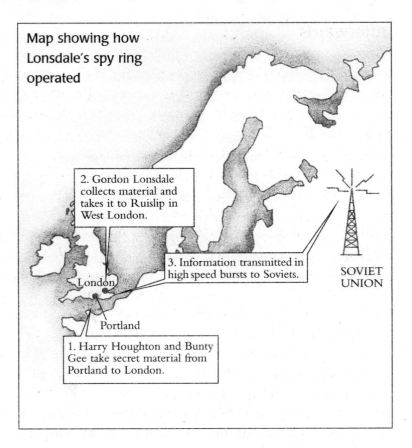

Map showing how Lonsdale's spy ring operated

2. Gordon Lonsdale collects material and takes it to Ruislip in West London.

3. Information transmitted in high speed bursts to Soviets.

SOVIET UNION

London

Portland

1. Harry Houghton and Bunty Gee take secret material from Portland to London.

Standing in the dock, Lonsdale smiled. He knew he would not be behind bars for long; he was too valuable an agent. In the tit-for-tat world of Cold War espionage he would soon be swapped for a captured English spy. His friends in the KGB would see to that for sure.

Afterwards

Lonsdale was right to be confident. Within three years he had been exchanged for the British spy Greville Wynne (see "The salesman and the superspy", pages 89-104). Back in his home country he was greeted as a hero, and showered with medals. He continued to work for the KGB, although he was now too well known to be sent abroad as a spy. But the stress of his double life in espionage caught up with him and he died young. In October 1970, aged only 48, he had a fatal heart attack while gardening at his Moscow apartment.

The Krogers had to wait longer for their release, but their KGB masters did not desert them. A British lecturer in Moscow was arrested on fake charges in 1969, and exchanged for them. Both of the Krogers lived to a ripe old age, Helen dying aged 79 in 1992, and Peter dying aged 84, in 1995. Later occupants of 45 Cranley Drive dug up yet another of the Krogers' radios in 1981, when they were gardening.

Bunty Gee and Harry Houghton had no one but each other to look after them, and they stayed in prison for nine years. They were released in 1970, six years being taken off their sentences for good conduct. They married in Poole in 1971, and ran a guesthouse in Brankscome, Dorset, under false names. Both of them are believed to have died sometime in the 1980s.

Double agent for the Czar

Desperate times breed desperate men. In the decades before the communist revolution of 1917, Russia had more than its fair share. There were fanatical revolutionaries willing to sacrifice their lives to further their own beliefs. There were supporters of the Russian monarchy, prepared to exercise terror to hold on to their own positions.

In such circumstances there are always people ready to take cold-blooded advantage of the uncertain age in which they live. People like Yevno Azev. Described by a biographer as "one of the most depressing characters in the history of the Russian Revolution", he was happy to betray and destroy anyone who crossed his path. Unlike many spies, who are motivated by strong moral or political convictions, Azev cared for only one thing – money.

His tale begins in Grodnensky province, Russia, in 1869. Born of poor Jewish parents, Azev, like all Russian Jews, faced a life of persecution. Despite the grinding poverty of his childhood, young Azev was bright, and did well at school. But when he left in 1890 he would not settle, and drifted from one job to another. Like many young Russians he dabbled in the fashionable left-wing politics of the day, and in 1892 signed a political manifesto denouncing Russia's ruler, the Czar. This fell into the hands of the Okhrana, the feared state secret police. When the Okhrana began to arrest all those who had signed this document, Azev was forced to flee. He ended up in Karlsruhe, Germany, where he enrolled at the local college to study electrical engineering.

Many of Azev's fellow students were also Russian exiles. He became friends with a group belonging to a political party called the Social Democratic Society, which he joined. Here he met young men and women who were violently opposed to the Czar's regime, and were prepared to give their lives in the struggle to depose him. Unfortunately for them, they met in Azev someone who was all too happy to help them on their way.

So poor he was starving, Azev was desperate to make some money. He wrote to the Okhrana, offering to spy against these revolutionary students. The Okhrana investigated him, and liked what they found. A report stated:

"(He) is intelligent and a clever intriguer. It can be assumed that his greed for money and his present state of need would make him zealous in his duties."

It was a wise assessment. Azev began to receive a wage – 50 roubles a month – which would allow him to live in some comfort. Shrewdly, he hoarded most of his income, and still lived a very frugal life. Whenever he did spend money, he told fellow students that he was receiving help from Jewish charities, to see him through his education.

❖

With a foot in both sides of Russia's political divide, Azev's career blossomed. Within the Social Democratic Society he took up a paid position, organizing and coordinating various revolutionary groups among anti-Czarist exiles throughout Europe. On his travels he came across an even more radical organization called the Union of Social Revolutionaries, and joined it. Meanwhile, making his way from one country to another, he sent back vast sheaves of information to the Okhrana about the Czar's exiled opponents in Europe.

So impressive were Azev's reports that he came to the attention of the Okhrana's chief, a man called S.V. Zubatov. He recognized Azev as a person of considerable cunning and a total lack of morality – someone much like himself, in fact – and he was determined to make more of this prize agent. What he had in mind was using Azev as an *agent provocateur* – someone who works among revolutionaries, persuading them to commit violent acts, so they can be discredited or punished. Zubatov knew he could pay Azev more than anyone else, so he felt totally secure in his loyalty.

On Zubatov's orders, Azev returned to Russia in 1901, and was given money to move to Moscow to mingle with anti-Czarist revolutionaries. He soon became a popular and trusted member of a group called the Social Revolutionaries, and quickly revealed details to the Okhrana of its leading members, and the location of a secret press which was used for printing revolutionary leaflets and posters. The press was raided and arrests were made, but no suspicion fell on Azev. Instead, the Social Revolutionaries blamed this misfortune on their own poor management and promoted Azev to put matters right. The Okhrana were so delighted that they doubled his salary. Azev rewarded them by betraying the head of his organization. After the head was arrested, Azev's salary went up a dizzy ten times its original level.

The Social Revolutionaries appointed a new leader, a fiery young man named Gershuni. He trusted Azev completely, and together they planned the formation of a terrorist squad which they called the Combat Section. It was here that Azev took his role as an agent provocateur a little too seriously. The first task allocated to the Combat Section was the assassination of Dimitri Sipyagin, Russia's Minister of the Interior.

❖

Despite the fact that he was an employee of Russia's Czarist government, Azev had no qualms at all about planning the assassination of one of its most important ministers. After all, what better way could he prove his loyalty to his fellow revolutionaries? Still, he figured, the Okhrana would not be very happy with one of their own agents killing a government minister. He would have to hoodwink them too.

So, in the week planned for Sipyagin's assassination, Azev took a trip out of Moscow. This way he could tell the Okhrana plans had been changed in his absence, and that he had had no time to warn them of the plot.

On April 5, 1902, a member of the Combat Section duly turned up at the Ministry of the Interior. He was dressed in an officer's uniform, complete with sword and pistol, and carried an envelope which he insisted he must personally deliver to the minister himself. He was ushered into Sipyagin's office and handed over the letter. It was a sentence of death. As the increasingly alarmed minister read the letter, he was shot at his desk.

Shortly after the killing, Azev slipped the assassin's name to the police, and this man was arrested.

Azev continued to play this extraordinarily dangerous game. His fellow revolutionaries expected more assassinations, and Azev obliged. His Okhrana employees expected warning of any violent revolutionary activity. Azev gave them enough names to keep them happy, but withheld enough information to be able to continue with his own terrorist activities.

Those Azev betrayed were carefully chosen – anyone who challenged his authority within the Combat Section, or who might learn of his association with the Okhrana. Naturally, Gershuni was selected. He was arrested and sentenced to life imprisonment in a Siberian slave camp. The Combat Section was devastated by this reversal of fortune, and elected Azev to be their leader instead. It was a fine promotion, for now Azev controlled the organization's funds too. Like his Okhrana salary, much of this was squirreled away for the future.

❖

Despite a gradual thinning of the bravest and best of their ranks, the Combat Section chalked up some spectacular successes – some of which were reported all around the world. With Azev pulling the strings and plotting the assassinations in great detail, they managed to dispatch Nicolai Bogolepov, the Minister of Education, N.M. Bogdanovich, Governor of Ufa, and N.I. Bobrikov, Governor of Finland. Azev always apologized to the Okhrana for being unable to notify them of such attacks in advance, but always delivered the names of the assassins after the deed was done. But just to allay Okhrana suspicions, he set up the assassination of Dimitri Trepov, the Moscow Chief of Police, three times. Each time he sent his men to kill Trepov, he tipped off the Okhrana first, and the assassins were arrested before they could carry out the deed.

In 1904, Azev planned the Combat Section's most daring move yet – the assassination of Sipyagin's successor at the Ministry of the Interior, Vyacheslav Plehve. As the minister drove through the streets of St. Petersburg in a horse-drawn carriage, a small, dark man raced across and lobbed a small package into Plehve's lap. What happened next was witnessed by a London journalist, who sent this report to his newspaper:

"Suddenly the ground before me quivered, a tremendous sound of thunder deafened me, the windows on both sides of the broad street rattled and the glass of the panes was hurled onto the stone pavement. A dead horse, a pool of blood, fragments of a carriage and a hole in the ground were my rapid impression."

Plehve was quite a target. A brutal and much hated minister, he had been responsible for the ruthless killing of many of the Czar's opponents, and had banned all political gatherings and meetings in Russia. He was also a fiercely anti-Jewish bigot, and had done much to ban Russian Jews from good jobs and housing.

Azev, of course, cared little for Plehve's political record, even his anti-Jewish racism, just as long as he was getting money from both sides. Once again he apologized to the Okhrana for not being able to prevent the assassination, but passed on the names of those who had carried it out.

More killings followed – another Moscow Chief of Police, a leading Jewish politician, even Grand Duke Sergei, the Governor General of Moscow, and Uncle to the Czar. But Azev also took care to continue to plan assassinations which would be discovered at the last moment, thanks to a tip off from him.

❖

Then things started to go wrong. In 1905 an anonymous letter was sent to a member of the Combat Section, denouncing Azev as a police spy. The Social Revolutionaries held a secret tribunal with Azev in attendance. He bluffed his way out quite coolly. Fellow revolutionaries lined up to defend his character, telling the tribunal that it was absurd to label a man responsible for the deaths of the czarist Minister Plehve and Grand Duke Sergei as a police spy. The charges were dismissed.

It was a lucky escape, but Azev's confidence had been undermined. The source of the anonymous letter was still a mystery. He felt secure enough with the Social Revolutionaries, so he guessed his betrayer must work for the Okhrana. Further disasters followed. The Combat Section's best bomb maker blew himself to pieces. Then the Okhrana seized their entire stock of dynamite. He had certainly not told them about it, which led him to suspect that there was another agent working among them. Perhaps he was being spied on himself? Then, potentially worst of all, an Okhrana agent defected to the Social Revolutionaries, bringing with him the names of two of its members who were spying for the Okhrana.

One of the names was the man he suspected had been sent to spy on him. He was killed immediately. The other name was Azev's. Once again his luck held, and he managed to convince his colleagues that he was on their side.

Shortly after this, Azev was attacked in the street by two thugs. They stabbed him fiercely, and he only escaped serious injury because his fur coat was too thick for the knives to penetrate too deeply. Azev was shrewd enough to realize this was a warning from the Okhrana, to remind him of where his real loyalties lay. His relations with the Okhrana were further soured when another revolutionary group tried to kill the Russian Prime Minister, Peter Stolypin. The strain of his double life became too much, and he closed down the Combat Section and fled to France.

"I have been in fear of my life since the days of Gershuni," he announced. "I have a right to rest."

❖

But life was too interesting to pass Azev by. In early 1907, Gershuni arrived back in St. Petersburg, having escaped from his Siberian prison camp in a barrel of pickled cabbage. Working under a false name, he resumed the Social Revolutionaries' campaign of terror, and the Okhrana pleaded with Azev to return to work. The opportunity to top up his now considerable fortune proved too much for him to resist.

Once back in Russia, Azev arrived to find Gershuni planning the assassination of the Czar himself. He reported this to the Okhrana, who promptly arrested 28 conspirators. Gershuni, meanwhile, conveniently died. His health had been ruined by his time in Siberia. Coming back to the stresses and strains of life as a violent revolutionary finished him off.

Azev now took the plot into his own hands, warning his fellow revolutionaries that planning and preparing for such a high-level assassination would be immensely expensive. The Social Revolutionaries duly organized a series of fund-raising efforts. Azev siphoned off the money to his own account and continued to pass on the names of revolutionaries to the Okhrana.

Various plans were put forward. A young priest who had joined the revolutionaries volunteered to kill the Czar. A group of bombers said they could blow up the Czar's private train. Then a plan was put forward to assassinate the Czar when he went to Glasgow, in Scotland, to launch a Russian cruiser which was being built in a shipyard there. This particular plot seemed like the best one, and Azev even went to Glasgow to supervise the assassination. But a young sailor who had volunteered to carry out the killing changed his mind at the last minute.

❖

Azev's days with the Social Revolutionaries were numbered. One of their members, a mild-mannered historian named Vladimir Burtzev, had long suspected Azev was a police spy. He carried out his own investigations and discovered that Azev was suspiciously wealthy. When Burtzev contacted a retired Okhrana officer who told him Azev was their top informer, the game was up.

Burtzev put his evidence before another Social Revolutionaries tribunal, which was held in Paris. Azev, still reluctant to give up the source of his rapidly growing fortune, was foolhardy enough to attend. Evidence was once again produced against him, but this time his own alibis and excuses were proved to be false. Azev was asked to return to the tribunal the next day to hear further evidence against him, but he knew his life was now in great danger. The prospect of a wealthy retirement beckoned, and Azev vanished into the back streets of Paris, deserting the revolutionaries he had led so spectacularly and betrayed so heartlessly.

Afterwards

In 1909, Azev fled to Germany clutching a handful of fake passports – a leaving present from the grateful Okhrana. He took with him a German cabaret singer he had met in Russia, named Heddy de Hero.

The couple settled under one of their many fake identities in an elegant quarter of Berlin. Azev became a member of the Berlin stock exchange and set about investing his money and other peoples' – something he did extremely successfully. For a few years all went well. Azev and Heddy blended into Berlin society perfectly, entertaining new friends in a home that was laden with silver, cut glass and at least one grand piano.

Then in the summer of 1912, on a visit to Frankfurt, Azev was sitting on a park bench when, quite by coincidence, Vladimir Burtzev sat down next to him. After Azev had got over his initial shock, the two men fell into conversation. Azev tried to convince Burtzev he was not a traitor after all, and told him: "If you hadn't reported my relationship with the Okhrana, I would have been able to assassinate the Czar."

But Azev knew Burtzev did not believe him, and would report their meeting directly to his fellow revolutionaries. Soon assassins would be sent to Germany to track him down. He and Heddy were forced to give up their plush Berlin stockbroker life and go into hiding. Two years later they returned to Berlin, but Russia and Germany were now at war. Azev had invested all his money in Russian stocks and shares, and these were now worthless. The fugitives were broke. Heddy remained by his side, but worse was to come. In 1915, Azev was arrested as a suspected terrorist and thrown into prison for two and a half years. When the war between Russia and

Germany ended he was released, but his health had been seriously damaged. In April 1918 he went into a hospital with a kidney complaint, and died within a week.

Azev had been one of the most successful double agents in history. He had played both sides against each other and won. But his achievements went unnoticed. He was buried on April 26, 1918, in a Berlin cemetery. Heddy de Hero was his only mourner.

After the Russian Revolution in 1917, Okhrana files were inspected by Russia's new communist masters. Lenin and others had thought of Azev as one of the great revolutionary leaders of the 1900s, and were deeply shocked to learn of his double-dealing treachery.

High living in Lisbon

Most spies are anonymous "little" men who blend into the background, and do their often deadly work unnoticed and unremembered. As William Colby, head of the CIA during the 1970s, once remarked, "the ideal spy is a grey man who has a hard time catching the eye of a waiter in a restaurant."

Not so Dusko Popov — such was the high-living, gambling lifestyle of this handsome ladies' man, that speculation continues to this day as to whether he was the role model for Ian Fleming's famous fictional spy, James Bond.

Much of Popov's life seemed to be straight from the pages of a racy novel. On one evening in 1941, for example, he was standing casually by a roulette table in the smoky grandeur of Portugal's Estoril Casino. A blonde woman next to him slid three chips onto the green baize. The numbers she chose were 22, 18 and 15. She looked up and caught his eye. He nodded. Then she placed a fourth chip on zero. Popov nodded again. The roulette wheel spun and a hush fell over the people gathered at the table as the ball clattered around the slots in the wheel.

Popov didn't really care where it landed. The important activity for him had taken place before the wheel had spun. The woman, who was the personal secretary to the head of German military intelligence in Portugal, was not really gambling. She was arranging a meeting between Popov and her boss. The first number was the day, the second the hour, the third the minute – 18:15 (6:15pm) on the 22nd of that month. The fourth number told Popov where that meeting would be. Following a pre-arranged code, zero meant Lisbon.

As he always did, Popov waited to see where the ball would land. He knew from past experience that the woman was an unlucky player, and this time was no exception. He smiled to himself and left the building, looking around to make sure no one was following him.

❖

Popov lived a complicated life and one that required a quick wit capable of remembering exactly who he was supposed to be, with any of the people he came into contact with. That night he had been meeting the Germans. They had employed him to spy on the British and Americans during World War Two. But Popov was actually a double agent, working for exactly the people the Germans were paying him to spy on. He had to stay on his toes.

He had been born into an aristocratic family in the Yugoslavian port of Dubrovnik, which is now in Croatia. Popov was a textbook playboy. Wealthy enough not to work, he spent his days meandering between Europe's most glamorous hotels and resorts, mixing with some of the wealthiest and most influential people on the continent. But there was more to Popov than nightclubs, casinos and an endless succession of girlfriends. He was bright enough to speak most European languages, he had a taste for adventure, and he had a strong sense of what was right and what was wrong. And as far as Popov was concerned, the Nazis were most definitely wrong. When World War Two broke out in 1939, he was in his element.

It was the Abwehr (German Secret Service) that first approached him. His contact with the organization was an extremely rich German friend named Johnny Jebsen. He and Popov had known each other since their college days together. After one student prank, Jebsen had arranged for Popov's release from police custody, and now he was hinting strongly that Popov could pay him back. Jebsen asked him to provide a list of Yugoslav politicians who would be willing to work with the Nazis, if Germany invaded their country.

It was an ill-judged approach, given Popov's views on the Nazis. Although he agreed to his friend's request, he went immediately to some acquaintances who had contacts with the British secret service. Put in touch with them, he reported what he had been asked to do, and offered to work for them as well. The British knew a sparkling opportunity when they saw one, and were more than pleased to make use of him. He became an agent in the XX (Double Cross) system, run by spymaster John Masterman, and was given the codename "Tricycle."

❖

Now it was Popov's turn to approach Jebsen. He told Jebsen that he had a friend in London who was willing to spy for the Germans. Popov also suggested that he could set himself up in neutral Portugal, posing as a businessman in the capital city, Lisbon. From there he could make regular journeys to London, to collect secret material from his agent there, and maybe even recruit others to spy on the British. The Germans thought that this was a wonderful idea. This was how he ended up arranging his secret meetings via roulette chips in the casino at Lisbon.

The whole scheme, of course, was an elaborate hoax. What Popov really wanted to do was pick up information from the Germans, deliver it to London, then bring back misleading reports for the German secret service.

It was a highly dangerous game, but it worked like a charm. Popov set himself up in Lisbon in 1940 where he made contact with the head of German intelligence there, a man named von Karsthoff. He duly set off to London, returning with a batch of bogus documents from his non-existent spy, all carefully concocted to mislead the German secret service. On one of his trips from London to Lisbon, Popov was accompanied by Ian Fleming, who worked for British Intelligence. (It was this meeting that led people to believe Fleming had based his character James Bond on Popov, an idea Fleming always denied.)

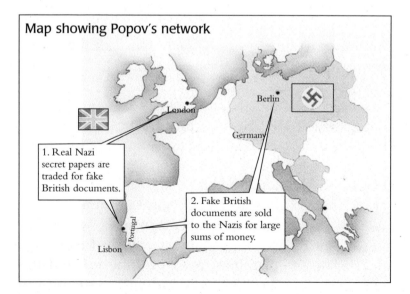

Map showing Popov's network

London

Berlin

Germany

1. Real Nazi secret papers are traded for fake British documents.

2. Fake British documents are sold to the Nazis for large sums of money.

Portugal

Lisbon

When von Karsthoff's bosses in Berlin read the documents he brought back from London, they were delighted. Popov was immediately rewarded with $10,000, which was then a huge sum of money. Popov carried on playing this game for a year and a half, and the Germans lapped up everything he brought them.

But Popov was not quite as clever as he thought he was. His friend Johnny Jebsen had discovered Popov was also working for the British. If Jebsen had revealed this, it could have led to Popov's torture and execution, but Popov was a very fortunate man. Jebsen's friendship with him was stronger than any political or national loyalties, and Jebsen did not betray him. Besides, Popov sensed his friend was becoming as anti-Nazi as he was, although they never discussed this openly.

Jebsen now began to alert Popov whenever his colleagues at the Abwehr made routine checks on Popov's activities. He also passed on to Popov any interesting news that he heard in Berlin. One piece of gossip Jebsen picked up was that Germany's ally Japan was planning to launch surprise air attacks on American Navy bases. The information was rather vague, but astonishing. Many people had suspected that Japan was planning to attack America, and this seemed to confirm that they had every intention of doing so.

These reports seemed even more likely when von Karsthoff summoned Popov to tell him he was to be sent to America to form a spy ring there. At the time Germany and America were not yet at war, but America was a strong supporter of Britain, one of Germany's greatest enemies. Among other tasks, he was to investigate how well prepared America's Navy was for war. Most particularly, he was to visit the Pacific islands of Hawaii to find out as much as he could about the Pearl Harbor Navy base there.

Von Karsthoff also had something interesting to show Popov.

"Look at this," he beamed with obvious pride. "These, Herr Popov, are something never seen before, and quite remarkable."

Then he took out a small box full of tiny black rectangles, each one no bigger than 2mm.

"These are microdots, Herr Popov. You are the first agent to be supplied with them. You have to pick them up with tweezers, and they contain pages and pages of information, which can only be seen under a microscope. A page of a document is photographed and the film is reduced to this minuscule size. You can hide them, of course, very easily – under a stamp of a letter, even under your skin – look, they are no bigger than a freckle."

Popov was impressed, and wondered what the British and Americans would make of this marvellous new technology. Von Karsthoff dismissed him with a hearty slap on the back.

"Once you are in America, Herr Popov, we will send you all the equipment you need to make these microdots," he said.

❖

So it was that Popov flew to America in August 1941, armed with $20,000 (now worth around $400,000) with which to set up his spy ring. The war was gathering pace. Barely two months before, the Germans had invaded the Soviet Union. The Soviet armies had crumbled before them, and now the German army was heading for Moscow.

Such news distressed Popov, as it would anyone who hated the Nazis, but he consoled himself with the thought that his trip was going to cause no end of trouble for the Germans. The news he carried about Pearl Harbor was nothing short of sensational. Also, he was presenting the Americans with a golden opportunity to set up and control a German spy ring on their own doorstep. This they could then monitor closely, and feed with false information to confuse the Germans. And, with the microdots, he was bringing along the very latest piece of Nazi high technology espionage equipment. Surely, the Americans would welcome him to their country with open arms?

But they didn't – Popov's spell in America brought only intense frustration. As soon as he arrived he made contact with the FBI (Federal Bureau of Investigation), a branch of the American government which, among other duties, was concerned with anti-spying activities. They refused to let him recruit any spies. They were immensely suspicious of Popov, and wanted to control any bogus spy ring themselves. They threatened to arrest him if he even tried to go to Hawaii on a bogus spying mission for the Germans. Worst of all, they refused to believe his warnings about a Japanese attack on Pearl Harbor.

"Your information is too precise," they told him. "It spells out exactly where, when, how, and by whom we are to be attacked. If anything, it sounds like a trap."

Most of all it was J. Edgar Hoover, the director of the FBI, who disliked Popov. Hoover was a strange, repressed and prudish man, who took an extremely dim view of what he saw as "personal immorality" in other people. Popov, in his usual way, had launched himself onto the New York social scene in great style, buying a luxury apartment, visiting the most fashionable clubs, and acquiring several very glamorous girlfriends.

The two men met only once, and Hoover made his disapproval all too clear:
"I'm running the cleanest police organization in

the world. Then you come here out of nowhere and within six weeks you install yourself on Park Avenue and start chasing film stars. I'm telling you right now I won't stand for it."

What Hoover really wanted to do was to use Popov as a lure to catch other, real, spies. He could not understand that Popov was too useful a contact to waste in this way.

Popov stayed in the United States for long enough to see his predictions come true, for the Japanese did indeed attack the Americans at Pearl Harbor, on December 7th, 1941. Eventually, the FBI allowed Popov to recruit just one bogus spy. This man then began to transmit false information to Germany. However the FBI would not tell Popov what these messages said.

When the Germans sent a courier carrying Popov's microdot equipment to the United States, Popov had to beg and plead with the FBI not to arrest the man as a spy. This would have completely blown Popov's cover. It was the final straw. He had had quite enough of the Americans and the FBI, and demanded to be sent back to Lisbon.

❖

Popov's British contacts were unhappy about this move, especially as Popov had no idea of the content of the messages the FBI had allowed their bogus spy to transmit. If the Germans questioned him about these messages, they would soon become very suspicious. If they realized Popov was acting as a double-agent, he would be tortured and killed. But Popov insisted on returning to Lisbon. His British secret service contact, Lt. Commander Ewen Montagu, called this "the greatest instance of cold-blooded courage" he ever saw. And Popov got away with it too.

Back in Portugal there were furious exchanges with von Karsthoff. What did Popov have to show for all the money he had been given? Where was his spy ring? However Popov gave just as good as he got, angrily telling von Karsthoff he had not been given nearly enough money to carry out his mission properly.

But there was good news too. Popov's Abwehr friend Johnny Jebsen arrived from Berlin to greet him. For the first time, Jebsen openly admitted that he had turned against the Nazis. During the time that Popov had been in America the Germans had invaded Yugoslavia, and Jebsen now suggested that the two men help to set up an escape route for Yugoslavs who wanted to flee from the Nazis. They intended to take them secretly across the Mediterranean sea to Lisbon, and then from there on to London. This was a very round about route, but by then most of Europe was under the control of Nazi Germany.

The scheme was a great success, and around 150 people were smuggled out. But when one of the escapers went missing between Lisbon and London, Popov and Jebsen feared the Nazis had sent one of their own spies on their escape route, and wondered if they had been betrayed.

On one of his trips to London, Popov discovered that this was exactly what had happened, although he did not know if he and Jebsen had been uncovered personally. His contacts in England begged him not to return to Lisbon, but once again he took a huge risk and went back. He was especially interested in returning because he wanted to recruit his friend Johnny Jebsen to spy for the British.

❖

When Popov arrived back in Lisbon, he went at once to von Karsthoff's office to make his usual report. When he got there he found that von Karsthoff was out, and he was asked to wait. Popov immediately began to suspect that something was wrong. On this occasion he had brought a pistol with him, and he was all set to use it at the first hint of trouble. He waited nervously in the office, staring out of the window. Then he heard von Karsthoff's voice behind him.

"Turn around slowly, Popov, and don't make any sudden moves."

Popov's blood turned to ice. He had been betrayed. He was about to reach for his pistol to shoot his way out when he noticed von Karsthoff's reflection in the window. There was a monkey on his shoulder.

"An agent from Africa gave it to me," von Karsthoff laughed. "He's not tame yet and might bite if he's frightened."

❖

Close escape or not, that incident appeared to be an omen. It seemed as if Popov's luck was finally running out. He did meet with Johnny Jebsen again, and successfully recruited him as a British spy. But in the weeks that followed, there were very clear clues that the Germans were on to him. One afternoon, Popov's car blew up shortly after he parked it on a beach. Then, after a successful evening at a casino, he found his latest girlfriend searching through his belongings. But still he hung on.

Finally, he heard that Johnny Jebsen had been betrayed by a colleague, and arrested. Popov could tempt fate no longer. He caught the first plane he could back to London, where he was to stay for the rest of the war.

Afterwards

Johnny Jebsen died in the hands of the Gestapo, a fate that could very easily have befallen Dusko Popov. After the war, Popov settled in Britain and became a British citizen. He continued living life to the full, as he had always done. He became an international business man, winning and losing a series of fortunes on business interests extending from Europe to South Africa. He published an account of his wartime experiences called *Spy/Counter Spy* in 1974. His second wife, with whom he had four sons, did not know of her husband's wartime exploits until she read his book. Later in life he settled in the South of France, and died there in 1981, aged 70.

The playboy sergeant

It was late 1960. Jack Dunlap, wife by his side, was talking to some new friends in the bar of one of Washington's swankier restaurants.

"I'm just an ordinary guy who got lucky," he said. "There I was pulling $100 a week in the military, with a nice little desk job ferrying around documents. I even worked evenings at a gas station for a dollar an hour to make ends meet. Five kids costs a lot of dough. My wife Diane here doesn't work either — too much to do at home. Then I inherited this plantation in Louisiana from a great uncle. I hardly knew him — how about that! I still keep my old job though — it's important for a man to have a job, don't you think?"

Jack's friends were impressed by his modesty and down-to-earth appreciation of his good fortune. Still, no one would have guessed he was a humble messenger for the US Army. Why, his outfit alone must have cost a couple of weeks pay. And that Cadillac outside — Elvis Presley himself would have been proud to drive it.

But catch Jack on another night, in other company, especially his statuesque, blonde mistress, and he'd have another tale to tell.

"Hey," he'd brag to her quietly, in the smoking room of some exclusive yachting club, "I shouldn't be telling you this, but I'm not who I say I am. My title at the Agency is 'clerk-messenger', but you should see some of the stuff I get to look at, and some of the jobs they ask me to do. . ."

His girlfriend would listen wide-eyed, and pump him for more details.

"I can't tell you anymore, baby," he'd crack. "If you knew what I actually did, I'd have to kill you."

"Boy," he thought, "was she impressed!" Actually, she knew he was just bragging. He seemed too ordinary to be the person he was pretending to be, but she didn't care. Jack had set her up in her own little apartment, and he took her to all sorts of exciting places – speedboat races, exclusive clubs, out in his cabin cruiser. Where he got his money from was none of her business.

❖

The real Jack Dunlap was a sergeant in the US Army. Every working day he checked into Fort Meade – the National Security Agency's labyrinthine headquarters in Washington. The NSA, as it was known, was America's top intelligence-gathering organization. The building itself was vast – its main corridor was the length of three football fields. Its walls contained more electrical wiring than any other building in the world. Its basement housed the most powerful computers then known to man. Its roof sprouted radio antennae which collected information from all over the world. Surrounding it were three rows of electrified barbed-wire fences, patrolled around the clock by armed marines.

Dunlap's job was indeed "clerk-messenger". He had to collect files from one department, then trundle down the corridors with his trolley, to another. Often the material he handled was highly sensitive – "raw" top secret messages on their way to be encoded before they were transmitted to Embassies and undercover agents all over the world. But Dunlap was considered to be a water-tight security risk. He had fought with great bravery in the Korean War and had the medals to prove it. He had been serving in the Army for eight years with no blemish on his record. He did his job with such quiet efficiency and little fuss that even if people recognized his lanky frame they often had trouble putting a name to it.

❖

In 1960 the Cold War between the USA and the Soviet Union was at its peak, and the Soviets were prepared to pay a small fortune to find out what went on in the endless, echoing corridors of the NSA. One night a Soviet agent who had discovered Jack Dunlap's daytime occupation approached him. They fell into conversation, and Jack was in an expansive mood. Yes, agreed the agent, five children were a terrible expense, especially on the kind of money the US Army paid their clerical staff. Still, he suggested, perhaps he could help Jack out financially – quite handsomely – in return for information? The huge sum of $50,000 per year was offered. This was nearly ten times what Jack was currently earning, and he told the agent he could count on him.

❖

Smuggling information out of the NSA was surprisingly easy. Jack slipped documents he was supposed to deliver under his shirt. Then he had them photographed or photocopied by a Soviet agent who worked in Washington. It was a piece of cake. One time he even took his mistress with him, although he didn't tell her he was delivering US secrets to the Russians.

Bizarrely, no one at the NSA seemed particularly concerned about Sergeant Dunlap's lavish new lifestyle. They swallowed his story about the plantation hook, line and sinker. So he drove his flashy new cars to work, and regaled workmates with tales of his new cabin cruiser and speed boat, and nobody thought to check him out more thoroughly. The Agency even gave him days off work for speedboat racing. When he injured his back in a regatta, they sent an ambulance to bring him back to a military hospital.

His friends were awestruck at this VIP treatment. Dunlap played the situation up to the hilt.

"They were afraid the sedatives might make me tell a lot of secrets I know," he confided.

But in March 1964 Dunlap's term of duty with the NSA came to an end and he was due to be posted elsewhere. What was he to do? How would he manage without his extra income? More to the point, how would he explain to his wife, and every one else, that he no longer had it. Dunlap had become used to his luxuries. Life was good and he wanted to keep things the way they were.

As he pondered, he realized there was a way around this problem. Dunlap told his bosses he and his family were too settled in Washington to move, and he would like to remain in his post at the NSA. He offered to resign from the army, if he could rejoin the Agency as a civilian.

As far as they were concerned, Dunlap had worked well and efficiently, and they were happy to let him stay. After all, the NSA did employ plenty of civilians. But there was a snag. Army personnel were considered above suspicion, but civilians had to pass a series of tests, including a session on a lie detector, before they could be taken on. Jack protested to his commanding officer.

"Look, I've been with this organization since 1958. Do I really have to go through this rigmarole?"

"Sorry Sergeant," the officer said. "Rules are rules. If you come back as a civilian, you gotta jump through all the right hoops. Anyway, you're a war hero, you're the right stuff, you won't have any problems."

❖

Dunlap brooded. He started to get anxious. He'd had such an easy ride he wasn't used to dealing with hitches. Then he started to psych himself up, wandering around giving himself a pep talk.

"Hey!" he told himself, "I've been smuggling out those documents for nearly four years. I'm cool – there's not been a sniff of bother in all that time. There's no way superspy Jack Dunlap is going to fail that lie detector test."

But he did.

They sat him down in a little office with a machine that measured his heartbeat, respiration and perspiration. Then they asked him a lot of questions, taking a careful note of how his body responded to each and every one of them.

The test results were damaging. They pointed to a character capable of "petty thievery" and "immoral conduct". The fact that Dunlap was committing high treason rather than stealing office stationery says a little about the limitations of the lie detector, but from that moment on, his life took a turn for the worse.

Dunlap was allowed to keep working as normal, but his poor showing in the lie detector test led to further investigations. NSA agents delved into his financial affairs and soon discovered there was no such thing as his Louisiana plantation. His income was obviously coming from an illicit source.

Nothing was said for two whole months. Dunlap was having sleepless nights wondering what was going on, and what his bosses did and didn't know about what he'd done. He knew things would be very serious if the scale of his treachery became known. Spies had been sent to the electric chair for less. Even if he escaped the death penalty, he would probably spend the rest of his life in a top security prison. Either way, the future looked bleak.

Finally, with no explanation, Dunlap was moved from his job ferrying confidential documents, and given more mundane clerical work to do. He was sharp enough to realize he was now in serious trouble. He rang his Soviet contact, but the man refused to see him.

"Don't call again," he told Dunlap menacingly. "You're on your own now."

❖

Work became a nightmare. When he arrived every morning Dunlap had visions of himself being carted off by burly security guards, and his wife and mistress reading about his betrayal in the newspapers the next day. When were they going to pounce? The strain was becoming unbearable.

In June 1964, Dunlap went to a stock car race with friends, and hinted that he was going to kill himself. Nobody believed him, but the next day they found him barely alive, having taken an overdose of alcohol and sleeping pills.

Another month went by, and nothing happened. The manner of his arrest continued to torment him. Would it be an early morning knock at the door, and a squad of heavily armed soldiers? Or would a silent, sinister man come up to him in the corridor at the NSA and whisper: "Mr. Dunlap, will you come this way please?"

He was beginning to crack.

On July 20, while at work, he tried to shoot

himself. But a friend on duty pulled the gun away from him just in time. Dunlap told him he was having "woman trouble", and wanted to end it all.

Two days later he finally succeeded. Driving to a deserted creek in one of his flashiest cars, he wound up the windows and suffocated himself with the car's exhaust fumes. His body was found the next morning.

Afterwards

A month after his death, the NSA finished their investigations. Dunlap was right to assume they'd find him out – they had gathered enough evidence to prove that he was a spy. But officials were still in the dark about precisely what information he had given to America's enemies. They later admitted they never really knew which documents passed through his hands, and had had to assume that everything that went through Dunlap's section was now no longer a secret to the Soviets.

Dunlap's wife did what she could to help. She discovered a large number of government documents in their home, and turned these over to investigators. Some material from Oleg Penkovsky, the Soviet officer who had spied for Britain and America (see "The salesman and the superspy", pages 89-104) passed through Dunlap's hands, although there is no proof he was responsible for Penkovsky's betrayal and arrest. However, he certainly provided the Soviets with useful information on US coding machines and also told them how much the Americans knew about Soviet military strength.

Bizarrely, because the whole episode was so embarrassing, and because the investigation was so vague in its understanding of exactly what Dunlap had done, the NSA kept the whole scandal secret. Dunlap was buried as a serving US Marine in Arlington Cemetery, in Washington. His grave was only a stone's throw away from the spot which was soon to become President J.F. Kennedy's final resting place. In a strange twist of fate, one of America's greatest heroes ended up lying next to one of its most damaging spies.

The Venlo snatch

It was October 21, 1939, and World War Two had just begun. In Zutphen, a town in neutral Holland, rain drummed down on the roof of a large Buick limousine. Behind the wheel Sigismund Best adjusted his monocle and squinted through the window of his car. Suddenly another car drew up. A man jumped out. Best leaned over to open the door and the man climbed in beside him. The Buick roared into life and rolled through the streets, wipers flailing.

Best looked like the typical English gentleman. Tall, with an aristocratic manner, he wore spats and a tweed suit. His hair was carefully oiled; he even wore a monocle. But this was deceptive. Best was in fact half Indian. He was also a spy. He lived in Holland with his Dutch wife, and ran a small business importing bicycles, but really he was a member of Z Branch – an independent group of agents which formed part of Britain's Special Intelligence Service (SIS).

Best's credentials were impressive. He spoke four languages, and during World War One he had run a successful network of spies behind enemy lines. Currently, he was trying to make contact with dissatisfied Germans willing to fight against Hitler and the Nazis. As far as he could tell, things were going very well indeed.

Best had been contacted some weeks earlier by one of his agents, a refugee who had fled from persecution in Germany. The man knew many high ranking officers within the German army and he had assured Best that there was a great deal of resentment against Hitler, resentment which had built up to a strong resistance movement. Best had probed deeper and had been given the name of an officer involved with the resistance movement – Hauptmann Schaemell. This was the man now sitting in the car with him.

Best spoke German well, and the two men drove through the Dutch countryside chatting together in German about classical music. At the town of Arnhem, they picked up two of Best's colleagues, an English officer named Major Stevens, and a Dutch officer named Captain Klop. Although Holland was neutral at the time, Klop was assisting the British. He wanted to keep his nationality a secret, so he was pretending to be Canadian and was using the name Coppens. This was a convincing alias. Klop had spent several years living in Canada, and the country was an ally of Britain's.

Best drove on. Schaemell, he reflected, seemed like a good catch. As they drove, the German reeled off a list of officers who were eager to see Hitler's downfall and named an important general who was prepared to lead the resistance. Schaemell promised to bring the general to their next meeting, which they set for October 30.

❖

What Best didn't know was that the Germans were one step ahead of him. The refugee who had introduced him to Schaemell was in fact a German spy named Franz Fischer. The resistance movement Best was hearing all about did not exist. Schaemell himself didn't exist either. He was really Walter Schellenberg – a 29 year-old ex-lawyer who was now head of German foreign intelligence. Instead of spying for Best, he wanted to annihilate him.

Schellenberg's plan was simple. Over the coming weeks, he intended to lull the British and Dutch agents into a false sense of security, by pretending to be a willing collaborator. Then he would lure them into meetings, which would enable him to penetrate the SIS and find out about their operations.

First, however, Schellenberg had to convince Best that he was genuinely working against the Nazis. When he returned to Holland from Germany on

October 30, he brought with him two army friends. One of the men was silver-haired, with an old-fashioned elegance which made him look as if he might be a disgruntled aristocrat seeking to overthrow the Nazis. It was a plausible disguise – many upper class Germans did regard Hitler as a common upstart.

They crossed the border and drove to Arnhem, where Best had agreed to meet them. But Best was not there. They waited. After three-quarters of an hour, they were about to give up when they saw two figures approaching their car. But these were not the British agents they were expecting. They were Dutch police officers, and they got into Schellenberg's car and curtly ordered him to drive to the police station.

This was not at all what Schellenberg had been planning. He was meant to be hoodwinking them, and now it looked like they had caught him instead. The head of German foreign intelligence was quite some prize.

There at the station Schellenberg and his army friends were given a thorough going over. Their clothes and luggage were searched from top to bottom, and this was nearly their undoing. In the wash-bag of one of Schellenberg's accomplices, open on the table ready for inspection, was a small packet of aspirins. Unfortunately for the Germans, these were not any old aspirins. They were a type issued to the SS (*Schutzstaffel*), the elite Nazi military corps, and bore the official label *SS Sanitaetschauptamt* (the main medical office of the SS). When Schellenberg spotted the pills, he turned white with alarm.

Thinking quickly, he looked around the room. Fortunately for him, the police officers searching their luggage were preoccupied with another bag. So Schellenberg swiftly snatched the aspirins and swallowed the lot – wrapper and all. The bitter taste was still in his mouth when there was a knock at the door. It was Klop, alias Coppens, Best's fellow agent. Schellenberg could only fear the worst.

❖

But Klop had come to rescue them. He apologized profusely for the trouble they had been put to. It was all an unfortunate misunderstanding, he assured them. But Schellenberg was no fool. He knew exactly what had been going on. The British and Dutch still suspected them, and this whole exercise had been a test to see if they could expose the Germans. If the police had found anything suspicious, such as the SS aspirins, then they would have been arrested.

Schellenberg himself had an even luckier escape. The paper and silver foil of the aspirin wrapper prevented his stomach from absorbing the drug, which could have seriously damaged his body.

From then on, everything went smoothly for the Germans. They were driven to the SIS headquarters in the Hague, and wined and dined like visiting royalty. The next day, Schellenberg and his friends were given a radio set and a call sign. They were told to keep in contact by radio, and that a future meeting would soon be arranged. They all shook hands and were driven back to the German border.

Over the next few weeks Schellenberg was in daily radio contact with Best's group. Two more meetings were held, and he now felt confident that they had accepted him as completely genuine.

❖

But then a major fly landed in Schellenberg's ointment, and flies didn't come much bigger than Heinrich Himmler, head of the SS. There had been an assassination attempt on Hitler – a bomb had exploded shortly after he had left a Nazi party celebration in Munich. Hitler was convinced the SIS was behind the plot, and wanted Best and his men captured immediately.

Schellenberg protested strongly. This would ruin his carefully thought-out scheme.

"The British are completely fooled," he pleaded. "Just think of all the information I'll be able to wheedle out of them."

But Himmler was curt.

"Now you listen to me. There's no but, there's only the Fuhrer's order, which you will carry out."

So that was that.

❖

With no option, Schellenberg devised a plan. He had already arranged his next meeting with the British — at Venlo, a small town on the Dutch-German frontier. He now contacted Alfred Naujocks of the SS, and arranged for a squad of twelve SS men to accompany him. Schellenberg met the men for a hurried briefing, and they sped off to the border.

Naujocks, a thuggish character, was known as "the man who started World War Two". Two months earlier, he and a hand-picked squad of men dressed as Polish soldiers, had staged a fake raid on a German radio station on the German-Polish border. This gave the Nazis the opportunity to claim they had been attacked by the Poles, and an excuse to offer their own people, and the world, for invading Poland, which they wanted to turn into a German colony.

Curiously, Naujocks was not impressed with Schellenberg, and later described him as a "namby-pamby, pasty-faced little man." He wondered how he would cope with the unquestionably dangerous business they were about to undertake.

The rendezvous with Best was at two o'clock, at the Café Backus, which was situated in a strange no-man's land between the German and Dutch frontier posts. Schellenberg was very uneasy and ordered a brandy to steady his nerves.

Finally, at 3:20pm, nearly one and a half hours late, Best's Buick came into sight. It turned into an alley by the café. Best and Klop got out, and Stevens stayed in the car. Schellenberg walked over as if to greet them, but as he did so shots rang out and a car roared down the street. It was the SS who had been lurking on the other side of the border. They had driven straight over the barrier firing as they went. It broke all the rules of neutrality — Holland was not at war and German soldiers had no right to cross the frontier.

There was instant chaos. Klop drew a pistol and fired at Schellenberg who flung himself to one side.

The SS car pulled up at the end of the alley. There were soldiers hanging from its doors and two machine gunners perched on its front fender. Klop ducked and shifted his aim. He fired, then let loose another shot, narrowly missing Naujocks in the front seat of the car. He jumped out and returned fire from behind the open door, while his men scattered for cover, their guns blazing.

Naujocks ran up to Schellenberg and shouted in his face.

"Get out of this! God knows how you haven't been hit!"

Schellenberg ducked around the corner to avoid the shots and ran head-on into an SS soldier. Unfortunately this man had not been to the briefing and did not recognize Schellenberg. He assumed he was Best, as both men wore a monocle. The soldier grabbed him and stuck a pistol in his face.

"Don't be stupid," said Schellenberg, "put that gun away!"

There was a struggle and the SS man pulled the trigger of his gun. Schellenberg grabbed his hand and felt a bullet skim past his head. At that moment Naujocks ran up and told the soldier he'd got the wrong man – for the second time that day he'd probably saved the "namby-pamby" man's life.

Schellenberg peered around the corner and saw Klop making a break for it. He had been hit and was now trying to get away across the street, the spent shells pumping from his pistol as he fired. But it was no use. A burst of machine gun fire brought him to his knees, and he crumpled into a heap. As he fell, SS men swarmed over to drag Best and Stevens into their car. A couple of them stopped to pick up Klop too, bundling him into their car like a sack of potatoes, but he was already dead. The German cars sped off to their side of the border, with a roar of over-revved engines, burning rubber marks into the asphalt road.

In the moment after they left, a strange silence hung over the scene. Passers-by and border guards emerged from doorways and blockhouses, and stood open-mouthed and motionless. Engine exhaust, burning rubber and the acrid tang of spent bullet cartridges hung in the air. A few pools of red blood stained the road, glistening sickly in the fading autumn afternoon.

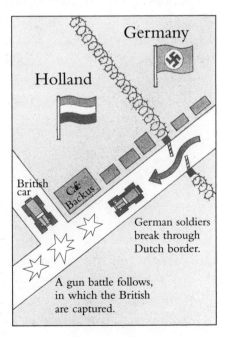

German soldiers break through Dutch border.

A gun battle follows, in which the British are captured.

The operation had been a huge success for Schellenberg. He had learned much about the methods of the SIS, and had obliterated Z Branch in Holland. A major threat to the Nazis had been put out of operation – and the war was barely two months old.

Afterwards

The Venlo incident was easily the British secret service's most embarrassing blunder of the entire war, and it had huge repercussions. Hitler used the event to justify the German invasion of Holland in 1940, claiming it proved that the Dutch were not really neutral after all. Furthermore, when Germans who were genuinely opposed to Hitler tried to make contact with British intelligence agents later in the war, they were treated with such suspicion that nothing ever came of their approaches.

Following their capture, Best and Stevens were interrogated at length by the Germans, and gave much away. Stevens was even carrying a list of all the British agents in Holland when he fell into the German trap.

Both men were sent to Sachsenhausen concentration camp where they remained for the rest of the war. They were freed when the camp was liberated by American soldiers in April 1945. Stevens died in 1965 and Best in 1978.

Schellenberg rose to become the head of Nazi foreign intelligence. After the war he settled in Italy, and died in 1952. Naujocks survived the war too, and died in 1960.

Behind the mask

Was there ever a spy more cunning than Richard Sorge? Regarded as one of the greatest secret agents of the 20th century, he led a double life from the moment he came into the world. His mother was Russian and his father was German; he was born in Baku, Russia, but raised in Germany.

Sorge was a fiercely patriotic German boy and, when the First World War broke out in 1914, he left his studies and volunteered for the army. He was sent to the Eastern Front where he fought bravely, receiving the Iron Cross (first class) for his efforts. But he also received shrapnel wounds to his legs which would leave him with a limp for the rest of his life.

As he recovered from his injuries back in Berlin, Sorge's view of the world began to change. He had lost faith in his youthful patriotism, but another ideology beckoned. He read the works of communism's leading writer, Karl Marx, and became convinced that this philosophy was the way to world peace and unity. By a curious coincidence, there was a family connection here too – Sorge's great uncle had been Marx's personal secretary.

When he was released from hospital, Sorge returned to his studies. He graduated from the University of Hamburg with a Ph.D. in political science. By now he was a committed communist and he worked hard recruiting students to his political cause. However, the German police suspected he was a communist spy and made plans to arrest him. Acting on a tip off, Sorge fled to Moscow. In 1917, Russia had become the world's first communist state, renaming itself the Soviet Union. Its leaders welcomed such an intelligent and diligent recruit to their cause. They were also charmed and fascinated to know of his family connection with Karl Marx, who had now become a figure of almost religious respect in the country. In Moscow, Sorge was trained as a spy, and taught to speak French, Russian and English. For the rest of his life, he would serve his mother's native country with unswerving loyalty and devotion.

❖

To begin with, Sorge was dispatched on spying missions all around the world. His most successful assignment was a four-year stint in the Chinese port of Shanghai. Here he found work as a freelance journalist for German newspapers – a very convenient cover for someone operating as a spy. The Soviet Union was eager that China become communist, and decided that Shanghai, with its huge foreign population, flourishing industry and world famous criminal community, would be the ideal starting point for a revolution.

Sorge was not a shrinking violet, and being inconspicuous was not part of his nature. He was a tall, fierce-looking man, who liked to drink, and was stridently independent in his dress and manner. He could be loud, rude, obnoxious even. Yet he had great charm too, and many people felt irresistibly drawn to him. Such a person made friends quickly, even in a strange land. Sorge soon had a network of colleagues and acquaintances that he could recruit to his cause. He hand-picked a group of American and Japanese residents in Shanghai, including Hotsumi Ozaki, a Tokyo journalist who would become a life-long friend.

For two years Sorge provided useful, if not earth-shattering, information, and proved he could work with great efficiency. But then Japan invaded and occupied China's northern province of Manchuria, which was on the Soviet Union's south-eastern border. Having an aggressive and effective Japanese army in its backyard caused great consternation in the Soviet Union. Sorge was recalled to Moscow. His commanders let him know they had been very pleased with his work in Shanghai, but now he was to be sent somewhere far more important – Tokyo. His mission was to find out whether Japan intended to invade the Soviet Union.

For a European like Sorge, Japan was one of the most difficult nations in the world in which to spy. The few westerners who lived there were highly conspicuous. They also had to learn a completely unfamiliar foreign language, and come to terms with some very different social customs. (In Japan for example, it is considered the height of bad manners to blow one's nose in public.) As a final obstacle, the Japanese were also highly suspicious of any likely spying activity. It was a tough assignment and one which required a long-term strategy.

Sorge began by inventing a suitable persona for himself. He would become a German journalist, and to do this effectively he had to return to his former home. But in Germany, Adolf Hitler and the Nazi party had recently come to power. They were fanatically anti–communist, and Sorge was sure that the Gestapo (Nazi Secret Police) would know about his days as a student communist in Hamburg.

Courageously, he returned anyway. Luck was with him. Perhaps his records remained untouched in the furthest reaches of some dusty police file? Perhaps a communist spy within the Gestapo had secretly destroyed the incriminating evidence? He never found out why he was not arrested.

Sorge asked editors with whom he had previously worked for references, and created a credible identity for himself as an ardent Nazi journalist, keen to work for the good of Germany and its new Nazi masters. He was so convincing the Abwehr (German secret service) even asked him to do a little spying for them. He quickly obtained a German passport and left for Japan in August 1933.

❖

Sorge knew he would have to stay in Japan for a long time. He spent the first two years there just getting used to this strange new country and its unfamiliar culture. He rented a small house, and immersed himself in Japanese life. He filled his home with Japanese books and art, slept on a low, Japanese bed called a futon, and left his shoes at the front door, in traditional Japanese fashion. To complete his education, he acquired a succession of Japanese girlfriends. While he was doing this, he dispatched a steady stream of newspaper reports that were to establish his reputation as one of Germany's leading foreign correspondents.

Friends in the German newspaper world provided letters of introduction to important people in Tokyo, and soon Sorge was a popular face at social gatherings for Tokyo's small but elite German community. As his confidence in his surroundings grew, he began to make contacts that would be useful for spying.

Sorge was made particularly welcome at the German Embassy, where officials were delighted to meet a fellow countryman who knew so much about the Far East. While Sorge would tell them all he could about China, they would fill him in on the latest stories about Japan and its foreign policy. Significantly, Sorge struck up a close friendship with a military attaché at the Embassy, Lieutenant-Colonel Eugen Ott. So believable was Sorge's loyal Nazi persona that Colonel Ott even allowed Sorge to travel with him on a fact-finding mission to Manchuria.

❖

As a spy Sorge was managing magnificently on his own, but his Soviet masters also wanted him to set up his own spy ring, so he began to recruit suitable members. The first, and most obvious candidate, was Ozaki Hotsumi. His old friend from Shanghai was now back in Tokyo, and still a journalist. Hotsumi did not share Sorge's faith in communism, but he was unsettled by his country's invasion of Manchuria and aggressive intentions towards the rest of China, which he saw as a threat to world peace. Like Sorge, he knew a lot of useful, influential people.

Also in the team was a Yugoslavian communist named Branko Vukelic, who worked as a photographic technician and journalist – both useful spying skills. Then Japanese-American Miyagi Yotoku was recruited. He had recently returned to Tokyo from California, and was an artist who made a small living selling his paintings. Finally, Max Klausen, a fellow German, was added to the team. He had worked with Sorge in Shanghai, and would be their radio operator, transmitting reports straight to the Soviet Union.

As a spy ring, it had its faults. Most of Sorge's fellow conspirators were foreigners. Even Miyagi, who was Japanese by birth, had been brought up as an American. He often found Japanese customs and conduct as baffling as the rest of them. Hotsumi, though, was invaluable. He managed to recruit informants in the highest circles of government. In his work as a journalist he became a special consultant to Prince Konoye, Japan's prime minister. While working with the Prince he was given access to masses of confidential information.

Sorge, in turn, was accepted at the German Embassy almost as one of the staff. They asked him to write reports, and gave him a small office where he worked as an unofficial secretary to the military attaché. In the privacy of this office, he photographed any document that was likely to be of interest to the Soviet Union. His position grew even stronger when his friend Eugen Ott was appointed German Ambassador. On one occasion, Sorge made plans to visit to Hong Kong, where he intended to deliver a batch of secret material to a Soviet agent. When Ott found out he was going, he gave him an equally secret batch of documents to carry safely to the German Embassy there. Sorge could not believe his luck.

❖

But spying is a very dangerous, difficult game. Once in a while, Sorge was careless. Shortly after he returned from Hong Kong, he was invited out for the evening by one of Tokyo's most important Germans – Prince Albert von Urbach. The two men visited several of the city's bars. By two o'clock in the morning, Sorge was seriously drunk and eager to go home. Rashly, he got on a motorcycle he often used to get around Tokyo, and roared off into the night.

Before long, he took a corner too fast, and crashed into a wall near the American Embassy. American security guards hurried over, saw Sorge bleeding and unconscious, and called the German Embassy. First to arrive to collect him was von Urbach himself. Sorge, now recovering consciousness, remembered he had several documents stolen from the German Embassy in his pockets. He muttered: "Tell Klausen to come at once." Fortunately von Urbach did as he was asked. Sorge stuffed the documents into Klausen's hand and passed out again.

The accident left him with some serious head injuries, and thereafter Sorge had difficulty moving some of the muscles in his face. Because of this, his expression would often become fixed, or contorted into an angry scowl – like that, said one friend, of a Japanese mask.

But as he recovered from his accident, Sorge's time as a spy was about to enter its most vital phase. In September 1939, Germany invaded Poland, and the Second World War began. This was particularly significant news for the Japanese government, as they were Germany's allies.

Sorge's masters were desperate for information about Japanese plans. The Soviet Union had signed a pact with Germany a month before the war began, with each side promising not to attack the other. But the Soviets were still deeply suspicious of the Japanese on their Manchurian border. Sorge's reply set them at ease. Japan, he told them, had no interest in the Soviet Union. Its real aim was to conquer China and defeat the Western powers – America, Britain, France and Holland – who had armies and colonies in the Far East.

But Sorge soon picked up other vital information which was deeply disturbing. He discovered that Germany had no intention of keeping its pact with the communists. When the time was right, Hitler planned to invade, and send his armies deep into the heart of the Soviet Union.

Such news was distressing enough, for someone as committed to communism as Sorge, but worse was to come — the authorities in Moscow did not believe him. Horrified, Sorge continued to pass on every snippet of evidence to back up his claim. By May 1941, he had conclusive proof — Germany had massed some 19 divisions on the Soviet border. They intended to invade in a month's time. Sorge even gave Moscow the exact date — June 22. But still, his spymasters, and especially the Soviet leader Joseph Stalin, continued to dismiss his reports as "doubtful and misleading information."

The invasion took place exactly as Sorge predicted. When he heard the news, along with everyone else in the world, from papers and radio reports, he broke down and wept. His Japanese girlfriend Miyake, who did not know he was a spy, found him sobbing in his study. She asked why he was so upset.

Sorge, feeling very vulnerable, was as honest as he could be without giving himself away.

"Because I am lonely. I have no real friends," he said sadly.

"But surely you have Ambassador Ott and other good German friends?" she said.

"Oh no. No, they are not really friends."

His face crumpled and he began to sob some more. Miyake waited expectantly, but Sorge would say no more. She knew him well enough not to inquire further.

But just as he was at his lowest ebb, Sorge was about to provide the most essential information of his career. With the invasion in full flow, German army divisions were pouring into the Soviet Union in great numbers. Soviet troops were fighting desperately against them. But large sections of the Soviet army were still based in Siberia, on the Soviet Union's eastern frontier. This was because Soviet commanders were sure that Japanese soldiers in nearby Manchuria would join their Nazi allies in the invasion of the Soviet Union. Sorge and Hotsumi once again scoured their sources for evidence of plans for such an attack.

In early October, Sorge sent a report to Moscow. Japan, he said, was definitely not going to attack the Soviet Union. This was the best news they had had since the German invasion began. Thousands of troops were rushed from Siberia to the west of the country to fight against the Germans. This decision almost certainly saved the Soviets from defeat.

But Sorge also told Moscow that Japan was planning an even more daring move. The Japanese

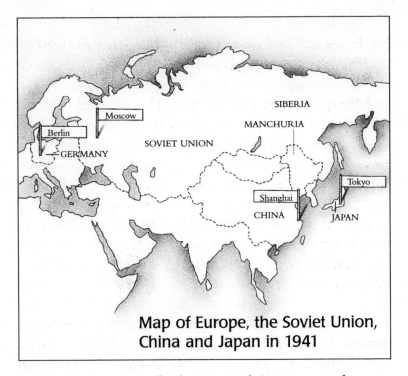

Map of Europe, the Soviet Union, China and Japan in 1941

were going to attack the United States navy base at Pearl Harbor. He even had a date, November 6, which turned out to be exactly a month too early.

❖

It was the last signal Sorge ever sent. In the previous month, the Japanese secret police had arrested several Japanese communists, whom they suspected of plotting revolution against the government. One of their suspects blurted out Miyagi Yotoku's name and he was rounded up a week or so later. It was a routine, almost leisurely operation, but it was to yield massive results. Miyagi was arrested and his apartment was searched.

Miyagi was not a robust man. He survived the first round of violent questioning without giving any secrets away, but decided he could take no more. The next day when police sat him down for another interrogation, he threw himself out of a window. Unfortunately for all of Sorge's spy ring, his fall was broken by a tree, and he only broke a leg. The next day, in terrible pain before the beatings even started, he confessed to everything, naming Hotsumi, Klausen and Sorge as accomplices.

For the Japanese secret police, this was a delicate matter. Sorge, the Ambassador's friend, was simply too important to be arrested. German–Japanese relations might be severely damaged, and this, after all, was a crucial time in Japanese history.

Sorge and Klausen were left alone, but Hotsumi was fair game. He was arrested and tortured. He too broke down, implicating Sorge, Klausen and the Yugoslavian, Vukelic.

Sorge was well aware something was going on. He had not been able to contact Miyagi or Hotsumi for several days, and feared the worst. He met Klausen and Vukelic to warn them, but they all decided to stay. Perhaps their previous successes had made them arrogant enough to think they would get away with it this time too, or perhaps they were just resigned to their fate?

Sorge went about his business as usual. He still met Ambassador Ott, he still worked on his newspaper articles, and he still went drinking at night in the bars of Tokyo. But the strain he was under was affecting his mental health, which was betrayed by the state of his house. It was so untidy it looked as if it had been robbed. Stale whisky, carelessly and regularly spilled over the floor, began to make the place smell like a seedy drinking den.

It was after one of Sorge's nights on the town that they came for him. Arriving home in a German Embassy car around five in the morning, he was watched by a squad of Japanese secret policemen. The Embassy car drove off, and a short while later the police broke down the door. Sorge was arrested in his dressing gown, whisky glass in hand. Klausen and Vukelic were picked up that same morning. All three had left sufficient evidence of their spying activities around their homes to make any denial a waste of time.

Japanese and German friends in Tokyo could not believe what had happened. Sorge himself tried to spin a story with his interrogators about being a double agent pretending to spy for the Soviets, while really spying for the Germans. But after six days of torture Sorge confessed. A secret trial of all of Sorge's spy ring followed. Klausen and Vukelic were sentenced to life imprisonment. Sorge and Hotsumi were sentenced to death. This was the first time a Japanese court had passed such a sentence on a European.

After the trial Sorge's life went into limbo. He spent several years at Sugamo Prison, where he passed the time writing a 50,000 word confession. Then, on November 7, 1944, almost three years after the death sentences had been passed, Sorge and Hotsumi were both sent to the gallows. The date was chosen to taunt Moscow. It was the twenty-seventh anniversary of the Russian Revolution.

Afterwards

Sorge was buried in an unmarked grave, but his Japanese girlfriend, Miyake Hanako, tracked down his remains and had him reburied alongside his friend Ozaki Hotsumi. Miyake remained devoted to Sorge, and even had a ring made from gold teeth extracted from his skull.

The Soviets remained strangely silent about Sorge and his successful spying mission for over 20 years. Then, in 1964, he was declared a hero of the Soviet

Union. A Moscow street was named after him, and his face was even put on postage stamps. Books and articles were published about his career. Two decades after his death, he was finally recognized as the brilliant spy he undoubtedly was.

The salesman and the superspy

Spying is a lonely game, and one which requires immense courage and patience. Many a spy has spent long, sleepless nights, wondering when his cover may be blown, and what terrible fate lies in store for him if he is betrayed, or gives himself away. A spy who is sent to uncover the secrets of an enemy country has troubles enough. But a spy who renounces his own country and seeks to work for an alien power faces almost certain torture and death if he is discovered.

Oleg Penkovsky was such a man. He was tall, handsome, and with an aristocratic courtesy and manner quite unusual in the communist Soviet Union. In 1960 he was a Colonel in the GRU – the Soviet Military Intelligence. Such was his rank he could move freely around the Kremlin, Moscow's fortress-like government headquarters, and had access to countless military secrets.

But Penkovsky eyed his world with a secret disdain. His father had been an officer in the Czar's army, and had fought against the communists in the

Russian civil war. Perhaps his family's opposition to Russia's new rulers had never really left him. Over the years he had come to hate the regime he served, and regarded Soviet leader Nikita Khrushchev as an oafish peasant.

At this time the world was embroiled in an era known as the Cold War. Although not actually at war, there were tensions between the communist Soviet Union, and western capitalist nations, such as the United States and the United Kingdom, who had become deeply suspicious of each other. Both sides built up their nuclear forces and engaged in a battle of propaganda and threats. Penkovsky was convinced that his country was planning to launch nuclear missiles against its capitalist foes, and the more he brooded, the more he began to wonder what he could do to undermine his masters.

Yet, as a young man, Penkovsky had been a model product of the Soviet system. He attended the prestigious Frunze Military Academy in Moscow, where he had been assigned to the GRU – an organization which accepted only the best recruits. His first spying mission was in Ankara, Turkey, in 1955. His cover was that of military attaché at the Soviet Embassy. Turkey was an ally of the Soviet Union's greatest enemy, the United States. The country shared a border with the southern Soviet Union, and the Soviets were anxious to find out as much as they could about Turkish military equipment and the US bases that operated there. Penkovsky was a very thorough, reliable agent, who carried out instructions to the letter.

Penkovsky returned to Moscow after a year, for further training. By 1960 he had been promoted to Colonel, although he was passed over for promotion to even higher rank because of his family's anti-communist record. Yet despite this, he was still trusted enough to lead a Soviet trade delegation to London, where, it was hoped, he would be able to set up a Soviet spy ring.

It was during the time when arrangements were being made for this trip that Penkovsky met a man who would have a major impact on his life. His name was Greville Wynne, and he was a British businessman.

❖

Wynne, who represented a British company manufacturing electrical goods, remembered the day he met Penkovsky quite clearly. It was a cold winter afternoon in an upper room at 11 Gorky Street, just off Moscow's Red Square. Wynne had been trying to persuade six Soviet officials to let a group of British businessmen visit the country. This was no easy task. At the time, relations between the two countries were very strained. Britain was a close ally of the United States. Suspicions raged on both sides. Still, life went on, and if a little trade could be arranged, then that might benefit both countries. Besides, trade, and trade delegations, gave both sides the opportunity to do some spying.

Wynne was not actually a spy, but like all western businessmen who visited communist countries, he was asked to keep his eyes open for anything the British secret service might find useful. Having served as a British intelligence officer during World War Two, Wynne was quite happy to cooperate.

That winter day in Moscow, the meeting seemed to be going well. Wynne had spent five years selling equipment in the Soviet Union and other communist countries in Eastern Europe. He was known to most of the men he was negotiating with here, and he thought they trusted him. By late afternoon, agreement was reached. In the Russian tradition, vodka was brought out to toast the arrangements.

As the men knocked back their drinks, they relaxed, and the conversation became more jovial. But Wynne's attention was drawn to one man he didn't know – he seemed better dressed than the rest of them, and had an air of authority. He drank very little and did not join in the general banter that passed around the table. That man was Oleg Penkovsky.

❖

Perhaps Penkovsky was keeping an aloof distance from his more junior colleagues, but his uneasy manner was also due to the intense anxiety he was feeling. In August that year he had passed a message to the American Embassy in Moscow, offering them his services as a spy. Now four months had passed, and there had been no reaction. What if the KGB – the feared Soviet secret police – had a spy in the Embassy, and Penkovsky's treachery had already been exposed? Actually, the Americans were extremely excited by his offer, but had been unable to find a safe way of getting back in touch with him. Perhaps, thought Penkovsky, Wynne or one of his colleagues would provide an opportunity for him to make contact with the West?

A month later, in December 1960, Wynne and a group of British businessmen arrived in Moscow on the business trip he had arranged at Gorky Street. Penkovsky was their official guide and he was waiting to greet them.

In the time they spent together, Wynne watched Penkovsky closely. He was sure the Russian had something on his mind, but the Colonel did not choose to confide in him. Instead, he approached another British businessman on the trip, who steadfastly refused to take any of the messages Penkovsky offered him.

This wasn't surprising – Westerners on such trips were warned to be careful of such approaches by seemingly friendly Russians, in case they become sucked into some KGB plot and exposed to blackmail. Penkovsky would have to wait some more.

❖

Wynne returned to the Soviet Union again in April 1961 to organize a return trip to Britain for Soviet businessmen. Once again Penkovsky was involved in the negotiations, and gave Wynne a list of names of those who would be going on the trip. His own name was right at the top.

"So you're coming too, Colonel?" said Wynne. His inquiring tone invited further disclosure.

"I am, Mr. Wynne," said the Colonel. Then he looked around to see who else might be listening, and his voice dropped to a low whisper: "But I have to say it is not for pleasure I come to London. I have many things to tell you."

With that, Penkovsky passed the startled Wynne a thick envelope. When he returned to his hotel, Wynne opened the packet. It contained details about

Penkovsky and his career, and a number of Soviet military secrets.

Penkovsky had chosen his man well. When they met the next day, Wynne took him to one side.

"I know people you can talk to," Wynne confided. "I'll arrange for you to meet them when you come to London."

❖

A few weeks later Penkovsky arrived in London with his delegation. They were wined and dined by British trade organizations, and enjoyed themselves immensely, shopping and taking in the capital's top tourist spots. Wynne acted as their guide. Then, every evening, after his colleagues had gone to bed, Penkovsky would be taken to a room in the hotel. Here he would be cross-examined by a team of American and British intelligence officers from the CIA and MI6.

They could hardly believe their luck. By the end of the first week Penkovsky had given them a mass of information, from the state of the Soviet Union's missile projects to the contents of the Kremlin phone directory. He was open about his reason for wanting to spy for the West, and convinced them that his main motive was his disillusionment with the Soviet regime. Penkovsky told his interrogators that he felt it was his mission to help maintain world peace. He also said he wanted to become a citizen of Great Britain or the United States, and be accepted as a Colonel in each of their armies.

The British and Americans were all too keen to oblige. In a ceremony set up especially for him, Penkovsky was sworn in as a citizen and colonel in both the United States and British army. Their man was a rare catch. He was a Kremlin insider of high rank. He seemed to be motivated by his conscience, rather than greed. He did ask to be paid for his work, but this was essentially to set himself up for his new life, which he envisaged taking up in the United States when his spying days were over. He did not ask for the normally outrageous sums requested for such information.

Yet, for all his obvious usefulness, both the CIA and MI6 had reservations about him. No one doubted his sincerity, or suspected he was a double agent for the Soviets, but some of his ideas were highly risky, or even ludicrous. He suggested, for instance, that they should plant a number of small atomic bombs in Moscow's military headquarters.

His character also caused concern. Penkovsky obviously saw himself as a hero who could single-handedly change the course of history. Above all, he told them he wanted to be remembered as "the best spy in history". Such vanity did not bode well for a long life.

❖

Penkovsky and his trade delegation returned to Moscow in May 1961, and his spying began in earnest. At Moscow airport his luggage was not searched. After all, he was too important a passenger to be bothered by such indignities. It was just as well. In one case he had hidden a miniature Minox camera and enough film for thousands of shots.

As he snapped his way though the Soviet Union's most sensitive secrets, Penkovsky arranged other trade trips for himself. He returned to London in July and visited Paris in September. On both occasions he met Western secret service officers to drop off his films. Altogether he delivered photographs of some 5,000 top secret documents. He also told his contacts, in fascinating detail, all that he had learned over nearly 25 years of service in the Soviet army and intelligence service. The CIA and MI6 had never known anything like it.

As well as his owns trips abroad, Penkovsky was also regularly visited by Wynne in Moscow. The British businessman acted as a courier, passing film between Penkovsky and the CIA/MI6 team, and bringing fresh rolls for the Minox camera. When

Wynne was unavailable Penkovsky was asked to make contact with Janet Chisholm, the wife of a British Embassy official in Moscow. This was a surprisingly safe arrangement. Like all Embassy officials Janet Chisholm's husband was under surveillance by the KGB, but Janet herself was not considered a security risk, and was free to come and go as she wished.

She met Penkovsky at a park in Moscow, taking her three young children along for the trip. Pretending to meet by chance, Penkovsky chatted amiably and naturally with her and the children, and then gave her a bag of fruit candy for them. If any one from the KGB had been watching, it would have looked like a harmless exchange of pleasantries, but the bag contained undeveloped film from the Minox.

❖

This risky game went on over the winter. Penkovsky met Janet Chisholm ten further times, but by the end of January 1962 he realized he was being followed. What he didn't know was that an American serviceman named Jack Dunlap, who worked for the National Security Agency, the top intelligence-gathering organization in the USA, was playing exactly the same game that he was (see "The playboy sergeant", pages 51-60). Reports from Dunlap to the KGB suggested strongly that Penkovsky was leaking secrets to the Americans.

On Wynne's next trip to Moscow, a very edgy Penkovsky confided that he was sure the KGB were on to him. Wynne passed this information on, and both the CIA and MI6 decided it was time to get Penkovsky out of Moscow. But how would they do it? One plan involved smuggling him out of Moscow airport inside a packing case. There was even talk of having him picked up by a submarine off the Baltic coast. While Western security services dithered, Penkovsky got more and more anxious, especially when he was refused permission to take trips abroad, a sure sign that he was under suspicion.

In July 1962, Wynne flew to Moscow on yet another trade mission. Returning one night to his hotel, he discovered that his suitcase had been searched. The KGB were on to him too. Three days later, he arranged to meet Penkovsky for an evening meal in a restaurant. As he arrived he noticed he was being watched by two men. Just then Penkovsky turned up too, but they could not find an empty table. Penkovsky turned and left, waiting for Wynne outside. The two men had a brief, hurried conversation.

"You are being followed. You must leave tomorrow on the first available plane," said Penkovsky, then vanished.

Wynne turned around to return to his hotel and immediately walked into the two men he had seen watching him earlier. Surprised to find themselves face to face with their quarry, they hurried away. Next morning Wynne went straight to the airport. He felt completely out of his depth. This was no situation for a businessman who had decided to dabble in a little spying. Penkovsky was there too to see him off with a desperate plea.

"Tell my friends that I must come out soon, very soon. I will carry on, but it is very dangerous."

❖

Wynne decided that it would not be safe for him to return to the Soviet Union, but in the autumn of 1962 he took a convoy of mobile exhibition trailers around several trade fairs in communist Eastern Europe. On November 2 he was in Budapest, the capital of Hungary. He spent an enjoyable evening entertaining prospective customers in an expensive restaurant, and then headed back to his trailers. Here, life took a considerable turn for the worse.

Four men stepped out of the shadows. They were all short and thickset, wearing identical dark suits and hats. They looked like a theatrical act, but what they did was far from entertaining. Wynne was grabbed by the arms and hurled into the back seat of a car. He shouted for help but a fist struck hard in his kidney, taking the breath from his body. A metal bar hit his head and a black shroud seemed to fall around him.

When Wynne recovered consciousness he was in a police station. The world seemed to swim around his eyes and he spent the next few days in a drugged stupor. He was taken to the Lubyanka, the KGB's headquarters in Moscow, the most feared prison in the Soviet Union.

Here, the KGB made a determined attempt to break Wynne's spirit. He was given a bare bunk to sleep on with only one blanket. An iron drum stood in the other side of his cell, for use as a toilet. Although it was winter, the guards would sometimes take away his blanket, and it was so cold he would freeze to his iron bed frame.

But all those business lunches, and the many evenings spent entertaining clients, had not softened the former wartime intelligence officer completely. Wynne was made of stern stuff, and he knew exactly what his captors were trying to do. He repeatedly insisted that he had done nothing wrong, and kept to his cover story, which was that he had been unwittingly duped into helping the British secret service. Despite all his ill treatment, he refused to sign a confession.

❖

The KGB had come for Penkovsky in October 1962, a month before Wynne had been kidnapped.

The two men saw each other for the last time at their joint trial in May 1963. The trial was a showpiece of Soviet justice. It was held in an elaborate courtroom where the judge sat beneath a huge, red and gold hammer and sickle – the distinctive emblem of the Soviet Union. Cameras rolled and journalists scribbled, as Penkovsky and Wynne stood in the witness box.

The judge gave his verdict. Wynne was sentenced to eight years imprisonment. As a Soviet citizen and traitor, however, his partner's punishment was to be much worse.

"Oleg Vladimirovich Penkovsky," the judge announced solemnly to the hushed, expectant courtroom, "guilty of treason to the Motherland, to be shot to death and all his personal property to be confiscated."

Whatever terrible tortures Penkovsky's interrogators visited on him in the last days of his life can only be imagined. His actual fate is still something of a mystery. It was whispered that when the KGB had extracted every last shred of useful information from him, they took the Colonel to a basement and fed him slowly, feet first, into an incinerator. Maybe that was just a story meant to frighten any other high-ranking Soviet officer who might be thinking of betraying his country. But maybe it was true. . .

Afterwards

After the trial, Wynne was returned to the dreaded Lubyanka. His treatment there was so harsh that on one occasion he had to be taken to a hospital, suffering from starvation. Then, in April 1964, he was suddenly dragged from his cell and put on a train and then a plane. He had no idea where he was being taken.

At 5:15am in the morning of April 22, 1964, a yellow Mercedes carried Wynne to Checkpoint Heerstrasse, on the eastern side of the border between East and West Berlin. At the same time, a black Mercedes drew up on the western side. Out of it stepped Konon Molody, the Soviet spy known by his alias of Gordon Lonsdale (see "This charming man", pages 7–22). He too had been captured and imprisoned, and he was now being traded for Greville Wynne. The two men walked across the border towards each other, and on to their own freedom.

The British government refused to admit that Wynne had been a spy, and did nothing to help him settle back into his disrupted life. He was treated far better by the Americans, who paid him $213,700, as compensation for his hardships. Unfortunately, he lost most of this money in unsuccessful property developments.

Wynne wrote two accounts of his adventures. Both books (*The Man from Moscow*, published in 1967, and *The Man from Odessa*, published in 1981) are said to be full of inaccuracies. He died in 1990.

Eye of the Morning

Fame and espionage seem an unlikely combination. Who would have thought that beautiful Margaretha Zelle, the Dutch-born dancer who had enchanted all of Europe in the early years of the 20th century, would make a suitable spy? In fact, who would have thought she would be remembered as one of the most famous spies of all time?

At the height of her fame as a dancer, she toured the capitals of Europe, from London to Rome, Vienna to Berlin. In Paris, such was her popularity that police had been called out to control the crowds that flocked to see her. She had a string of famous lovers, including the German Kaiser's son, Crown Prince Wilhelm. But Margaretha's fame was not like fame is now. In the days before television, and newspapers and magazines obsessed with celebrity life, her face faded soon enough in the memory of most men and women in the street.

Margaretha's life was anything but ordinary. Born in 1876 to a wealthy Dutch hat maker and his Javanese wife, she was spoiled as only a privileged, unusually beautiful child can be. But her mother died when she was only 14, and Margaretha was sent off to a convent. At 19, she married a Dutch army officer named Rudolph MacLeod. The couple went to live in Java (now part of Indonesia), which was then a Dutch colony.

Married life was far from easy for Margaretha. MacLeod was a brutal man who drank heavily, and was often unfaithful. He also tried to hoodwink acquaintances by setting them up in compromising situations with his wife, and then blackmailing them.

A son was born to the couple in 1896, followed by a daughter. The son was poisoned by a servant whom MacLeod had mistreated, and died. Shortly after this tragic event Margaretha divorced her husband and returned to Holland with her daughter.

❖

Margaretha, now approaching 30, was alone and penniless, and had no obvious way of making a living. But what she did have was a supple body and a vague memory of some Javanese dances learned during her time in the colony. And she was still stunningly beautiful.

Leaving her daughter with relatives, she set about completely reinventing herself. Margaretha Zelle left for Paris, and arrived there as exotic oriental dancer

Mata Hari, which means "Eye of the Morning" in Javanese. She soon found work in a prestigious night club, and became the talk of the city. Margaretha was also an accomplished ballet dancer, and appeared in acclaimed ballet productions. Nine years of celebrity followed, and famous or wealthy lovers who showered her with money and jewels.

But in 1914 World War One began, and Margaretha's merry-go-round life came to an abrupt end. She was in Berlin at the time, and returned home to Holland as soon as she could.

Life was so much drearier in wartime. Margaretha was now almost 40, and for the first time in her life she was bored. After two years of wartime in neutral Holland, stuck at home with nothing to do, she was desperate for excitement.

So she was in a particularly receptive state of mind when an unusual visitor knocked on her door one night in May, 1916. He was Karl Kramer, Press Attaché to the German Consulate in Holland, and he had a particularly unusual request. He sat down with her at the dining table. When he was certain they were alone, he began to speak.

"In all your years of fame," Kramer explained delicately, "you have known some of the most powerful men in Europe. Would you consider returning to Paris now to mingle again with these influential gentlemen? And, while you're doing this, might you be able to keep me informed of anything interesting they might say?"

Margaretha looked curious but non-committal.

Kramer went on, "We could pay you well for this information – say 24,000 francs."

Margaretha allowed herself to show a glimmer of interest.

"Possibly, Herr Kramer, possibly. 24,000 francs might do well enough."

But, inside, Margaretha was absolutely thrilled. She was missing the money and excitement of her previous life quite acutely. What could be more glamorous than being a spy?

❖

Kramer returned to her house a few days later, carrying a small leather case. Inside was 24,000 francs and three small bottles. Two held a pale, transparent liquid, the other a bright, blue-green substance.

Kramer explained, "This, my dear Madame Zelle, is invisible ink. Now watch this very carefully. First you dampen the sheet of paper with the fluid in the first bottle, then you write down any useful information for me with the liquid in the second bottle. Then you dab the blue-green liquid over the top and let it dry. . ."

Margaretha looked on with great interest. Kramer felt like a magician performing a magic trick.

". . . and then, you can write a more innocent letter over the top, telling me about the ballet you went to last night, or your dear little poodle or whatever. Then, when I get it, I sprinkle yet more chemicals on top, and the message underneath comes through quite clearly."

Kramer almost added, "Make sure you do it right though. If you're caught, you could be shot." But somehow, he felt, this would be an unwelcome dose of reality in Margaretha's world. He did give her a code name, however – she was to be known to him as "H21".

❖

Margaretha returned to Paris only with some difficulty. At this time, the border between France and neutral Holland was being guarded very carefully, and the border police were only letting people with special passes travel between the two countries. But Margaretha showed her worth at once. She knew many important people in France, and several letters from politicians and high-ranking army officers to the French Consulate in Amsterdam soon persuaded officials to provide her with the necessary pass.

Margaretha didn't take her spying career very seriously. To her it was just a game which allowed her to spend 24,000 francs. Some invisible ink reports filtered back to Kramer, but most of the time, Margaretha just enjoyed renewing old acquaintances and visiting the haunts of her glory days. Actually, she was having the time of her life.

But while she didn't take her spying very seriously, the French and British secret services did. They had received reports that she might be a German spy, and were watching her closely. But nothing she did gave them any cause to believe their suspicions were justified.

In Paris, Margaretha met a young Russian officer named Vladimir de Masloff and soon they were passionately in love. Then Vladimir, who was fighting alongside the French, was wounded on the Western Front. Margaretha was desperate to see him, but he had been sent to a hospital near the front, which was forbidden to civilians. Margaretha went at once to the French War Ministry, intent on getting a permit to visit her lover. When she got there she marched through the first door she came to. Before her sat an official at a large, important looking desk, and she began to explain why she had come.

What Margaretha didn't know was that the War Ministry building also housed the French Security

Service. By a strange quirk of fate, she found herself sitting opposite Captain Georges Ladoux, head of French counterintelligence – the agency set up to investigate foreign spies.

He knew all about Margaretha Zelle, and was quite aware that she might be a spy. Now here she was, sitting before him, telling him she wanted to visit a forbidden area. It was too good to be true. He played her along, and told her she would get her pass at once. When she had gone he immediately notified two of his agents, telling them to follow her and watch her like a hawk.

❖

Of course, Margaretha had wanted her permit only with the intention of visiting Vladimir. Ladoux's agents had nothing suspicious to report. So, after her return, Ladoux called her into his office. Like Karl Kramer, he too knew that she had friends in very high places, and he tentatively inquired if she might be able to travel to Germany and do a little spying for the French.

As far as Margaretha was concerned, this was all money for nothing. Fate was offering her another wonderful slice of good fortune. But, cool as ever, she looked him straight in the eye and asked him for one million francs.

Ladoux struggled to keep a straight face. That was more than he would pay a dozen of their best agents put together. He was frank with her.

"Madame Zelle," he said, "you are virtually unknown to us. We don't know if we can trust you, and even if we decide we can, I can pay you no more than 25,000 francs for your services."

Margaretha shrugged. It could be worse. Then she made an error so fatal she could have been signing her own death warrant. Eager to show Ladoux she would be value for money, she boasted:

"I know a man who can organize everything for me in Germany. His name is Kramer."

Ladoux knew him too. If Margaretha Zelle was familiar with him, then in all likelihood she was a German spy after all. Clearly, there was more to her than met the eye. He asked her to go back to Holland and await instructions.

❖

Margaretha returned home by sea, but en route her boat was stopped in the English Channel by a British ship. The British were searching for a dangerous German agent named Clara Benedict, and they had with them a photograph of the woman they were seeking. Unfortunately for Margaretha, she bore a close likeness to Clara, and she was arrested immediately and taken to England.

Two weeks of interrogation followed. After a great deal of shouting and unpleasantness, Margaretha convinced the British that she was the famous Mata Hari, and not Clara Benedict. But even then, she was not released. Her interrogator, Sir Basil Thomas, told her:

"I would be delighted to set you free, but something rather curious has happened. We have been in touch with our people in Holland, and they tell us that Madame Zelle, or Mata Hari, is suspected of being a German agent."

Margaretha's double dealings were catching up with her. She thought wildly, then burst out:

"I am not a German agent. I work for Captain Ladoux in Paris."

Thomas contacted Ladoux at once. "Never heard of her," came the baffling reply. Ladoux obviously did not want to admit to asking Margaretha to spy for the French.

Eventually, the British let Margaretha go. Thomas had her placed on a boat bound for neutral Spain, warning her that she was way out of her depth and playing a very dangerous game. But Spain was the worst place they could have sent her. Madrid was teeming with spies of all nationalities. Once again, Margaretha was penniless, only this time she was in a foreign country. She decided to buckle down and get some serious spying done.

Uncertain of whether to work for the French or the Germans, she decided to spy for both sides – after all, she reasoned, they had been stupid enough to let her do so before. To the French she gave reports of German agents landing by submarine on the coast of Morocco. To the Germans she passed on news of forthcoming attacks by French and British troops.

But all of her information was second hand, and no more than what each side was certain the other side already knew. The French and German secret services were just testing her, almost certain that she was working for both sides. Eventually the Germans lost patience. They had wasted 24,000 francs, and now they had had enough. They deliberately leaked information to the French, to confirm that she had been working for them.

❖

Margaretha was summoned to Paris. No sooner had she arrived than she was immediately arrested and sent to Captain Bouchardon of the French Secret Service to be interviewed at length. He had been expecting a legendary beauty, and was surprised to see Mata Hari looking tired and gaunt.

Tired she may have been, but Margaretha was not going to give up without a fight. As they talked she denied everything, trying frantically to offer explanations of her dealings with the German secret service. She even tried to pass off Kramer's 24,000 franc payment as compensation for some valuable furs she had left in Berlin.

Bouchardon looked at Margaretha Zelle and sighed. He remembered her as a fabulous, exotic dancer in pre-war Paris. How much had changed. Clearly, she was no longer the exotic beauty who had enchanted an entire continent, but she was still a striking woman, and Bouchardon was not immune to her charms.

Everything about Margaretha told Bouchardon that she was a bumbling amateur. Whatever information she had given to the Germans was almost certainly worthless, and she had been working for the French too. In another time they would have let her go home to Holland, with a stern warning never to come back to Paris. But the war was going badly for France. Millions of men had been killed and people were demanding scapegoats. Spies, it was said, were everywhere. An example had to be made. So it was decided that Margaretha was to be tried as a spy – a crime that carried the death penalty.

❖

On July 24, 1917, Margaretha Zelle stood before a closed military court. She was on trial for her life.

Her lawyer, an old lover who could not believe that she had been a traitor to France, hoped to call influential friends from her past as character witnesses to defend her. But the tide had turned against her. Nobody wanted to be publicly associated with a woman who was now perceived as a dangerous German spy.

The trial went badly from the start, although Margaretha defended herself bravely. As she had done with Bouchard, she tried to pass off evidence of German payments to her as compensation for lost belongings, or gifts from lovers. It all looked increasingly implausible. Yet equally implausibly, the prosecution described her as "one of the greatest spies of the century", and alleged that she was "responsible for the deaths of tens of thousands of soldiers". Margaretha listened to the accusations unbowed. But when the prosecution also revealed her secret German code name, H21, her resistance and composure collapsed. She began to panic and her whole body started to tremble.

It was all over in less than two days. Margaretha was found guilty of spying against the French and sentenced to death. In deep shock, she could not bring herself to believe her wonderful life had turned out so badly.

"It's not possible, it's not possible," she repeated over and over.

Margaretha watched the summer fade to autumn from her cell window. Appeals were lodged and rejected, and now a date had been set for her execution – October 15. She was to be taken to Vincennes, a chateau on the edge of Paris, and shot by firing squad.

She slept well the night before, and was woken by Captain Bouchardon at 4:00am. In her cell were two nuns, there to keep her company.

"It's not possible," she said again to them. Then, "Don't worry sisters. I know how to die. You'll see a good death."

She had decided she would leave the world as she had lived – with as much splendour as she could manage. She put on an expensive dress, some beautiful shoes, a fine shawl, a hat and long gloves. She seemed quite calm.

"Why do you have this custom of executing people at dawn?" she said to the nuns. "In India and elsewhere it takes place at noon. I'd much rather go to Vincennes about three o'clock, after a good lunch."

And so she continued for the final two hours of her life. She stepped out of the car that took her to Vincennes with as much dignity as she could manage, and walked confidently before the firing squad. She refused a blindfold and would not be tied to the stake set up for her execution.

It was over mercifully quickly. Twelve shots rang out and she slumped to the ground. As the morning mist lifted, the body that had once entranced a continent was loaded into a coffin and taken away.

Afterwards

Mata Hari continues to be an object of great fascination in the world of espionage. Plenty of photographs still exist showing the dancer in her sultry prime, and ensuring that she is still remembered over eighty years after her untimely death. Her stage name has become an all-purpose description for an attractive female spy. The Dutch Mata Hari Foundation, an organization set up to prove her innocence of the charges made against her, still hope that she will one day receive an official pardon.

Her story has been the subject of several films and, until the creation of James Bond, she was the classic symbol of glamorous espionage. Greta Garbo played her in a 1931 film called *Mata Hari*. Like many films, the truth is buried among the drama on the screen, which focuses on her love affair with Vladimir de Masloff. In the film, she sends news to her lover that she is dying in a hospital, rather than about to be shot. Another film of her life was made in 1985, this time starring Sylvia Kristel.

In the late 1990s Margaretha was in the news again, for a very bizarre reason. After her execution her head was preserved in a private museum, but it was stolen, and has so far not been recovered.

The allure of Mata Hari stretches into the 21st century, and recently a computer software package for seeking out hard-to-find Internet information was named after her.

The gentleman's gentleman

Ludwig Moyzisch was not amused. He had been woken from a deep sleep and summoned to the house of the First Secretary to the German Embassy in Ankara, Turkey. In the middle of the night. What could possibly be this important?

It was October, 1943. Europe was deep into World War Two. Neutral Turkey, uncomfortably positioned between Nazi-occupied Europe and Soviet Russia, was teeming with spies. Moyzisch, a member of the German secret service, the SD (Sicherheitsdienst), was one of these spies. He had a cover job as a trade representative at the German Embassy, and he was often expected to do odd, unexpected things at strange times of the day.

Nonetheless, he was even more irritated when he got to the house. The First Secretary had gone to bed, and it was his wife who greeted Moyzisch at the door.

"There's a strange sort of character in there," she said, pointing to the drawing room. "He has something he wants to sell us."

Then she too left for her bed, telling him to be sure to close the door properly when he left.

Moyzisch was seething, and walked briskly into the drawing room. He was determined to sort this visitor out as soon as possible. His eyes searched around the clutter and paraphernalia of the room, and it took a few moments before he noticed a still, pale figure, sitting stock still on a sofa, his face hidden in shadow. Something about this man made Moyzisch stiffen suspiciously. His temper receded, and he concentrated on clearing his head.

The visitor stood up. He was small and squat, with thick black hair and a high forehead. Moyzisch later recalled his face as being "that of a man accustomed to hiding his feelings", but on this occasion his dark, piecing eyes darted around the room, betraying his unease.

The man went over to the door, and suddenly jerked it open, to see if anyone was hiding behind it. Moyzisch's irritation returned. He was a spy, not one of the Marx Brothers, and this was not a silly film. But he kept his silence and let his visitor do the talking.

"I have an offer to make to you," the man began, talking in fluent but heavily accented French. "But first I must ask for your assurance that nothing I say now will go beyond you and your chief. If you betray me, your life will be as worthless as mine. I'll see to it if it's the last thing I do."

With that, he drew his hand across his throat.

Moyzisch looked at the man coldly. Certainly, he could not take a threat like that seriously. But he was a professional spy, and his training told him to wait and see what else this stranger had to say. It was certainly interesting. . .

"I can deliver to you photographs of top secret information – extremely secret information – from the British Embassy. But if you want it, you'll have to pay me a great deal of money. I'll risk my life for you, so I want you to make it worth my while."

Moyzisch spoke for the first time: "And what sort of sum would you be thinking of ?"

"I want £20,000 – sterling – in cash."

Moyzisch's mask slipped. He could not resist a sneer.

"That's completely impossible," he replied. "What on earth have you got that would be worth such a huge sum of money?"

In 1943, such an amount was a veritable fortune.

"Well, think about it," said the stranger. "I'll give you three days to decide. Then I'll call you at the German Embassy and identify myself as "Pierre". I shall ask if you have any letters for me. If the answer is yes, I shall come and see you. If no, then you shall never hear from me again. If you're not interested, there are others who certainly will be."

Something about this man made Moyzisch hesitate to dismiss him. He almost certainly meant to take his information to the Soviet Embassy in Ankara if the Germans turned him down, and he certainly did mean business. Moyzisch agreed to this arrangement and the man got up to leave. Just as he got to the door he turned and smiled slyly.

"I'll bet you're dying to know who I am. Well, I'll tell you. I'm the British Ambassador's valet."

Before Moyzisch could say any more the door slammed shut, and the strange little man was gone.

❖

The next morning Moyzisch arranged to see the German ambassador, Franz von Papen. The sum of money this man demanded was so huge they would have to ask permission to give it to him from the German Foreign Secretary, Joachim von Ribbentrop, himself. They were certain he would say no. But a reply came back accepting the arrangement. A special courier was being sent from Berlin with the money.

Moyzisch gave his stranger a code name – Cicero, after a famous Roman orator – and made preparations for his visit. Sure enough, the phone call from "Pierre" came and they arranged to meet at the Embassy at 10:00pm that night.

Moyzisch was well prepared. He arranged for a darkroom, complete with a photographic technician, to be made ready, so he could check the film on the spot. The strange man turned up right on time, and the two of them began a tentative, suspicious exchange. Cicero wanted the money first, and then he would hand over the film. Moyzisch wanted the film to check if it was genuine, then he would hand over the money. They came to a compromise. Moyzisch counted out the £20,000 in front of him, then returned it to the safe and took the film to the darkroom.

The results were spectacular: unquestionably authentic top secret documents, all with recent dates. Cicero got his money, and a further arrangement was reached whereby the Germans would pay him £15,000 for every subsequent delivery. The money was an astronomical amount, but then, the information was simply extraordinary.

❖

The next night Cicero returned again with yet more film. When he left he asked Moyzisch to drive him back to the British Embassy. The German was astonished.

"But why not?" said Cicero, simply. "That's where I live."

More films followed, each revealing documents containing highly sensitive information. The Germans could not believe their luck. Cicero was simply too good to be true, and they suspected he was playing a game of double-bluff with them, supplying fake information to confuse and mislead the German Secret Service.

Moyzisch was instructed to find out all he could about their contact in the British Embassy, and soon built up a picture of Cicero. His actual name was Eleyza Bazna. He was an Albanian who had made his way to Turkey and settled in Ankara. Here he found work as a chauffeur, then a butler, and then as a valet to high ranking diplomats. He had worked for the Yugoslav ambassador and a German diplomat who had fired him for reading his mail. Finally, he had found work at the British Embassy as the valet for a high ranking official.

Bazna was very good at his job. He was servile, efficient, and had a knack of being able to second-guess what his master wanted. He was intelligent too, and spoke several languages fluently. When the position of valet at the residence of the ambassador Sir Hughe Knatchbull-Hugesson came up, Bazna got the job.

What Sir Hughe didn't know was that his new manservant had several interests which were to prove quite counter-productive. One was photography, another was Mara, a maid at the Embassy, and the third was snooping around in Embassy files. When Bazna discovered how easy this was, it became a full time passion.

❖

Bazna found out that his new master was a man of punctilious habits. Everything in Sir Hughe's life was run like clockwork. He liked to bathe morning and evening, play the piano after lunch, and have his meals at exact times of the day. When he went out in his purple Rolls-Royce, he knew exactly when he was leaving and when he would return.

Another of Sir Hughe's habits could not have been more accommodating – he liked to read top secret documents in his residence, and kept them in a safe there.

One evening, while Sir Hughe was having his bath, Bazna slipped into his bedroom, on the excuse of laying out his evening clothes, and made a wax impression of the safe key. He then had a replica key made up by a friend. After that, everything Sir Hughe kept in his safe was given a thorough read by his manservant.

Such a routine was perfect, and the more Bazna snooped, the more daring he became. On one occasion, after Sir Hughe had taken a sleeping pill, Bazna even read and photographed his secret papers on a bedside table.

And what secrets they were! Plans to launch air attacks from Turkey against Nazi ally Romania. . . Details of meetings between the American president Franklin Roosevelt, British Prime Minister Winston Churchill, and Soviet leader Joseph Stalin. . . best of all for the Germans, Bazna passed on news of the forthcoming Allied invasion of Europe from England to France. Bazna even gave the Nazis its codename – "Operation Overlord".

But, bizarrely, the Nazis still believed such information was too good to be true. Although they thought Bazna was genuine, they assumed the information he was supplying was fake – deliberately planted by British intelligence for him to find and pass on to the Germans.

❖

Bazna cared little for what the Germans did with his information, and even less for what they thought of it – just as long as the bank notes kept coming in. The money was piling up. He made no great effort to hide it, and kept it under his bedroom carpet.

Not all of his ill-gotten gains were saved for a rainy day. Bazna began to spend extravagantly. A country cottage was rented and equipped with every modern convenience. In another alarming breach of secrecy, Bazna even called it "Villa Cicero" after his German code name, and had a little plaque with this put up above the door. He and girlfriend Mara became regular customers at the ABC Store on Ataturk Boulevard – the most fashionable shop in all of Turkey. Their clothes and jewels would have shamed high society socialites.

Moyzisch became irritated with the way Bazna flaunted his wealth, especially when he began to wear a gold watch. Even Mara, who believed he was working for the Turks, started to chide him.

"People are going to start to wonder about how we can afford such wonderful clothes. You're just a valet after all."

"Don't you worry," he smiled. "They're all too stupid."

But they weren't. Curiously, it was the Turks who first started to take an interest in Bazna. They were neutral in the war. As the conflict dragged on, they began to wonder which side it would best suit their own interests to support. One night, after Bazna had dropped off more film at the German Embassy, and Moyzisch was driving him home, they noticed a large black car was following them. Moyzisch slowed, the car slowed. Moyzisch speeded up, the car speeded up. Desperate to shake them off, Moyzisch hit the accelerator and sped through Ankara's fashionable boulevards at a death-defying 190kmph (120mph).

Later that week, Moyzisch bumped into a Turkish official.

"My dear man," said the Turk, "you really are a most reckless driver. You should take more care – especially at night."

It was a warning, and the first hint that Bazna's spying days were numbered.

❖

More alarming events followed. At the British Embassy a team of security experts arrived to install a security system on the ambassador's secret documents. But Bazna heard Sir Hughe discussing the system with one of these men, and was able to work out a way of bypassing it.

Secrets still continued to flow from the British Embassy to Germany, but Bazna was about to be given away by a spy of far greater daring than he. In the German Foreign Ministry worked Fritz Kolbe, a German who hated the Nazis. Kolbe had direct access to all the material that Cicero was supplying to the Germans in Ankara, and he alerted the Americans. The Americans then told the British that they must have a spy on the loose inside their Embassy.

But still British intelligence could not establish Cicero's identity. His eventual betrayer came from within the German Embassy. Moyzisch had a surly, deeply inefficient secretary named Nellie Kapp. She was blonde, 20 years old, and pouted and sulked her way through the working day. She was so lazy that Moyzisch really wanted to get rid of her – the only reason he didn't was that her father was a high-ranking German diplomat.

But curiously, Nellie, for all her faults, did at least show quite an interest in Moyzisch's work. This was because Nellie was also a spy. She worked for the American Office for Strategic Services (OSS) and had had a key cut to fit Moyzisch's safe. She too photographed everything that passed through it. Before long, she had a very good idea that Cicero was Eleyza Bazna.

❖

By the end of March 1944, Nellie had done her job, and decided it was time to escape. After all, if staff at the German Embassy discovered she had been spying on them, she would be tortured and then shot. She cut her hair, dyed it black, and took a plane out of Turkey.

Meanwhile, the British secret service was still not quite sure Bazna was their man, so they set a trap. One night a British security officer, Sir John Dashwood, settled down in Sir Hughe's office with a glass of whisky. He switched the lights off and waited. Soon enough, the door opened, the light came on, and there stood Bazna, key in hand. The two men looked at each other. Not a word was said. Then Bazna turned and left. It was all over.

Bazna could not be arrested, as he had broken no Turkish law. After a furious row with a spluttering, highly indignant Sir Hughe, he rounded up his possessions, including all the money under his carpet. Then he left the Embassy for good, to lay low in one of Ankara's more exclusive districts.

Moyzisch, meanwhile, was having a very uncomfortable time. His secretary had vanished under extremely suspicious circumstances, and now his best agent had been uncovered. His masters in Berlin were extremely displeased, and had sent him a stream of telegrams demanding his immediate return to Germany. Moyzisch feared for his life. To buy some time, he telegraphed back that he was ill, and could not travel. Shortly afterward, he received a phone call at his home.

"I'm calling on behalf of the British," said a mysterious voice. "If you go back to Germany you will be shot. Come over to us and save your life."

It was a terrible dilemma to be in, and Moyzisch was reluctant to betray his country. He was a loyal Nazi who had joined the party before Hitler came to power. Even now, he still believed in the Nazi's evil cause. But, fortunately for him, he never had to make the decision. Shortly after, the Allies did indeed invade France, as Cicero had predicted, and the war turned very definitely against Germany. The Turks took this as a cue to join the Allies. All German diplomats, including Moyzisch, were arrested and detained for the rest of the war.

Afterwards

Bazna was extremely pleased with himself. He was still alive, and he was fabulously rich. He took himself, and £300,000, off to Portugal, and then to South America. But here the world turned sour. Bankers turned up at a luxury villa Bazna had rented, and told him that all the banknotes he had placed with them were counterfeit.

Bazna took the news well. He laughed out loud at the Germans' deception. They had decided his information was useless, and they were not going to pay real money for it. But what followed was far from funny, at least for him. Bazna was arrested, and sent to prison for passing forged banknotes. When he was released he headed for Germany, and asked the West

German government to compensate him for his lost "earnings". Unsurprisingly, his request was not successful. He died, lonely and poverty stricken, in Istanbul in 1971.

Ludwig Moyzisch did rather better after the war. He gave evidence at the Nuremberg trials of Nazi war criminals and then returned to civilian life in Austria. Here he took up his bogus embassy alias for real – becoming an export manager for a textile firm. He wrote a book, *Operation Cicero,* about his spying activities, which was later made into a film called *Five Fingers,* starring James Mason.

Love conquers all, or does it?

It all seemed too good to be true. On August 12, 1961, Bogdan Stashinsky, the Soviet Union's greatest Cold War assassin, arrived at West Berlin's police headquarters and gave himself up. That evening, Stashinsky was grilled by an astonished group of high-ranking intelligence officers. The story he had to tell was not a pretty one.

Stashinsky was born in the Ukraine in 1931, when it was part of the Soviet Union. Many Ukrainians wanted independence and were in revolt against Soviet rule. Among them were members of Stashinsky's own family. Bogdan was different. He was a committed communist and to show his dedication he betrayed his relatives.

The authorities were impressed, and Stashinsky was soon recruited to the KGB, the Soviet Union's intelligence service. After two years training, he was given a variety of undercover jobs, hunting down anti-Communists in Soviet-occupied Eastern Europe. The KGB watched the progress of their

young recruit with interest. He was good enough to be assigned the riskiest of jobs. In 1957 he was given a mission worthy of his talents – the assassination of Ukrainian resistance leader, Lev Rebet.

❖

The KGB called Rebet the "Sly Fox" and he was a formidable opponent. Little was known about him. All Stashinsky had to go on was that he ran his resistance organization from Munich, an area of Germany that was outside the control of the Soviet Union. His secret headquarters were in a building known as "the bunker". He was a powerful man, quick on his feet, who wore glasses and hid his shaven head under a beret. He ran his organization with an iron fist. Anyone Rebet suspected of being a Soviet spy was shot without hesitation.

Unperturbed, Stashinsky flew into Munich and set to work. He began to stalk known meeting places of Ukrainian exiles, and within a few days he was certain he had identified Rebet. Now all he had to do was kill him.

❖

The weapon Stashinsky intended to use was a newly developed gas gun. It was a light metal tube which fired a poisonous spray which would kill within 90 seconds. The spray left no trace, and if used effectively, would give the impression that its victim had suffered a heart attack. The poisonous gas was so dangerous that Stashinsky had to take an antidote pill before he fired the gun, in case he caught a whiff of it.

It worked like a dream. Stashinsky caught up with Rebet on the stairway of an office block. He walked past him, hiding the gun in a bag of sausages, and squirted him with one swift movement. Rebet staggered back, and fell down the stairs. By the time his body was found, Stashinsky had slipped quietly away.

Stashinsky was hailed as a hero and rewarded with a special KGB banquet. A year later, the Soviet authorities decided another Ukrainian exile in Munich needed to be assassinated. His name was Stefan Bandera, and Stashinsky was the obvious man for the job.

One autumn day Bandera returned to his apartment, loaded down with groceries. As he fumbled with his door lock, a stranger approached. It was Stashinsky. He smiled and asked Bandera if his door key worked. Bandera looked puzzled, but saw the gas gun too late to react. Stashinsky fired it straight into his face, then calmly walked away. But this assassination was not so smooth. Bandera staggered off to get help, and died on the way to hospital. The West German police were in no doubt that he had been murdered.

❖

Discreetly or not, Stashinsky had done his job. Again, he was hailed as a hero, and given the KGB's highest award for bravery, the Order of the Red Banner. But just as his career was going so well, Stashinsky ruined it. While on assignment in Soviet-controlled East Berlin, he fell in love with a 21-year-old German hairdresser named Inge Pohl.

The KGB were appalled. They thought a love match from within the KGB would be far more suitable for their star assassin. But Stashinsky had made up his mind. The couple were married and he brought his new bride to live with him in Moscow.

Falling in love seemed to have mellowed Stashinsky. He confessed all to Inge and told her his work now sickened him. She was appalled and encouraged her husband to give up his grisly profession. She also told him she hated living in Moscow, and openly suggested the two of them defect to West Germany.

Alas, the KGB were watching Stashinsky and his new wife very closely – so closely, in fact, that they had bugged the couple's apartment, and were opening their mail. When Stashinsky found this out he was furious. The row he had with his commanding officer ended his career.

Inge, now pregnant, returned to her parents in East Berlin. Stashinsky was refused permission to follow, and told he must remain in the Soviet Union for the next seven years. A child was born, but died six months later. In these tragic circumstances the KGB allowed Stashinsky to visit his wife in Berlin, and attend the funeral.

It was too good an opportunity to miss. During the visit both Stashinsky and Inge slipped away. Using false papers they entered West Berlin, where Stashinsky gave himself up to the police. Here he confessed to the murders of Rebet and Bandera, and a high profile trial followed. In 1962 he was sentenced to 13 years in prison. But the spy who had given up his job for love was in for a shock. Inge Pohl divorced him in 1964.

Afterwards

Stashinsky was released from prison after serving only four years of his sentence. He vanished soon afterwards. It is thought he was taken to the United States where he could assume a new identity, far away from the KGB assassins who surely be sent to hunt him down. There is speculation that his ex-wife also joined him in the USA, and that their divorce was just a ruse.

More Usborne True Stories

SURVIVAL

PAUL DOWSWELL

As he fell through the floor, Griffiths
instinctively grabbed at the bombsight
with both hands, but an immense gust
of freezing air sucked the rest of his
body out of the aircraft. With the wind
and the throb of the Boston's two
engines roaring in his ears, he found
himself halfway out of the plane, legs
and lower body pressed hard against the
fuselage. He yelled at the top of his
voice: "Geeeerrrooooowwww!!!!", but
knew immediately that there was almost
no chance his crewmate could hear him.

From shark attacks and blazing airships to exploding
spacecraft and sinking submarines, these are real
stories of people who have stared death in the face
and lived to tell the tale. Find out what separates the
living from the dead when catastrophe strikes.

ESCAPE

PAUL DOWSWELL

Finally, the night had come to take a trip to the roof. Morris spent the day beforehand trying to curb his restlessness. What if the way up to the roof was blocked? What if the ventilator motor had been replaced after all? All their painstaking work would be wasted. The 12 year sentence stretched out before him. Then another awful thought occurred. The holes in the wall would be discovered eventually, and that would mean even more years added on to his sentence.

As well as locked doors, high walls and barbed wire, many escaping prisoners also face savage dogs and armed guards who shoot to kill. From Alcatraz to Devil's Island, read the extraordinary tales of people who risked their lives for their freedom.

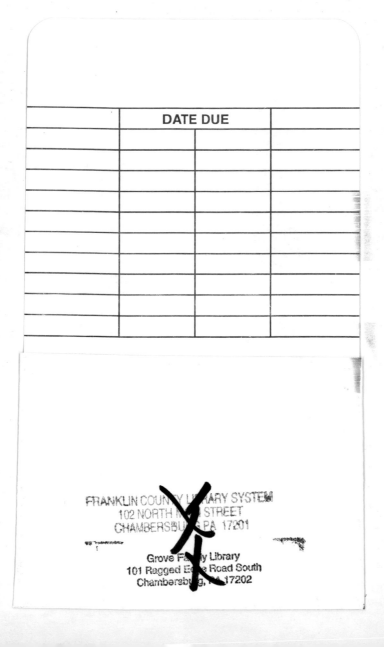

DATE DUE

More Usborne True Stories

HEROES

PAUL DOWSWELL

His blood ran cold and Perevozchenko
was seized by panic. He knew that his
body was absorbing lethal doses of
radiation, but instead of fleeing he
stayed to search for his colleague.
Peering into the dark through a
broken window that overlooked the
reactor hall, he could see only a mass
of tangled wreckage.

By now he had absorbed so much
radiation he felt as if his whole body
was on fire. But then he remembered
that there were several other men near
to the explosion who might also be
trapped . . .

From firefighters battling with a blazing nuclear
reactor to a helicopter rescue team on board a fast-
sinking ship, this is an amazingly vivid collection of
stories about men and women whose extraordinary
courage has captured the imagination of millions.